Letters to
MATTHEW

LIFE AFTER LOSS

LOUISE BATES

BALBOA.
PRESS
A DIVISION OF HAY HOUSE

Balboa Press books may be ordered through booksellers or by contacting:

Balboa Press
A Division of Hay House
1663 Liberty Drive
Bloomington, IN 47403
www.balboapress.co.uk
1 (877) 407-4847

Because of the dynamic nature of the Internet, any web addresses or links contained in this book may have changed since publication and may no longer be valid. The views expressed in this work are solely those of the author and do not necessarily reflect the views of the publisher, and the publisher hereby disclaims any responsibility for them.

The author of this book does not dispense medical advice or prescribe the use of any technique as a form of treatment for physical, emotional, or medical problems without the advice of a physician, either directly or indirectly. The intent of the author is only to offer information of a general nature to help you in your quest for emotional and spiritual well-being. In the event you use any of the information in this book for yourself, which is your constitutional right, the author and the publisher assume no responsibility for your actions.

Any people depicted in stock imagery provided by Getty Images are models, and such images are being used for illustrative purposes only. Certain stock imagery © Getty Images.

Scripture taken from The Holy Bible, King James Version. Cambridge Edition: 1769; King James Bible Online, 2018. www.kingjamesbibleonline.org.

Scripture quotations are from the ESV® Bible (The Holy Bible, English Standard Version®), copyright © 2001 by Crossway, a publishing ministry of Good News Publishers. Used by permission. All rights reserved.

Print information available on the last page.

ISBN: 978-1-9822-8057-4 (sc)
ISBN: 978-1-9822-8058-1 (e)

Balboa Press rev. date: 04/24/2019

This book is dedicated to everyone
who knew and loved Matthew.

*"I used to think that time was a healer, but I've realised now,
we are the healers and that time is just the
vehicle that takes us on that journey."*

DISCLAIMER

This book is based on my experience.

I understand that grief is a very personal journey and there are no rules.

I am not selling myself as a therapist; nor do I pretend to have the cure for grief, because there is no cure!

This book is not intended as a substitute for the medical advice of physicians. The reader should regularly consult a physician in matters relating to his/her health and particularly with respect to any symptoms that may require diagnosis or medical attention.

ACKNOWLEDGEMENTS

Thank you to my amazing best friend, husband and soul mate: Bill. You are my rock.

Thank you to the incredible human being that is my daughter, Sarah. You are my Guru!

I would also like to express my deep gratitude to my friends for proof reading the early drafts and giving me valuable feedback and encouragement. Thank you, Beth, Chris, Christina, Rebecca and Maidy.

"This book is incredible - honest, poignant and open, and it's going to help so many people".
Victoria Derbyshire, BBC Journalist, Television / Radio Presenter and Author

"Louise's book has the potential to inspire people who feel stuck in grief. By using various tools including EFT and Matrix Reimprinting, Louise has been able to courageously move through the grieving process in a very different way. A truly inspiring read!"
Karl Dawson, Hay House Author, Training Director EFT & Matrix Reimprinting Academy

"Everyone has a story to tell but not many people could share their experience of grief in the way Louise has shared hers. A heart breaking read with an uplifting, spiritual undertone. Inspirational!"

Nick Cooke, Therapist, Writer and Trainer. Creator of the Mindfulness Now Teacher Training Programme

PREFACE

So why have you picked up this book? Why would you want to read about grief and loss? The sadness revealed in the following pages of this book may bring you down and upset you. This book is not sugar coated, or light hearted, and it has not been edited to make it an easy read. I say this, not to put you off reading, but to make sure you feel safe when reading it. If anything in this book upsets you, or makes you feel uncomfortable, there is no shame in taking a break and reading something a bit more cheerful. Your mental health and wellbeing should come first after all.

Please keep in mind that what follows is my account of the experience of losing my son, from my perspective. Occasionally I will use poems, song lyrics, and even quotes from the bible that resonate with me. I am not a church person, but you do not need to be religious, or spiritual to benefit from these words; they are there to bring comfort and wisdom. I feel that these words are helpful and uplifting, and essential to bring in some balance and good energy to the pages. You can just enjoy them for what they are - kind, loving words.

Grief is one of the most painful and difficult experiences we encounter. It is something we might experience at any time during our lives and it can come as a sudden shock or it can be expected. Either way it is devastating.

Our ancestors were more familiar with death because so many of their children died young. That doesn't mean their grief was any easier, but they had more practice and they knew how to grieve. If we are very lucky, in the western world, we can go through most of our lives and not experience grief.

Family, society and religion can only do so much with their well-meaning ways, but they are not equipped to deal with the rawness of overwhelming sorrow and grief.

The British in particular have an unhelpful attitude to grief with their stiff upper lip and keep calm and carry on approach. Phrases like, "*keep your chin up*", "*don't mope about*", "*get over it*", "*your loved ones wouldn't want you to be sad*", "*you need to move on*" etc. are not what I wanted to hear.

My first experience of grief was losing my seventeen-year-old big brother when I was eleven and I have lost many relatives and friends since then.

When my son Matthew was seven, he witnessed a tragic accident when his school friend, who he was playing with, was run over and killed almost outside our house. Years later, he lost another friend, who was tragically killed while on patrol in Afghanistan. Individually and as a family we have experienced a lot of loss.

When my son Matthew died, my life changed forever. Nobody could have prepared me for the emotions, experiences and insights which followed his death. Losing him took me to a new level of grief. It was a dark place, darker than anything I had experienced in my life before.

For me grief felt like a trance which sucked me in. It felt like a vortex which consumed every part of me. It was brutal and all-consuming, but I knew it wouldn't always be like that. I experienced deep dark thoughts and feelings and emotions and for a while I lived there.

There were moments when I would be pulled out of this place, by a conversation with someone or maybe a television programme or some other distraction and, for a while, I would be somewhere else.

As time went on, more of these experiences would pull me out of this grief trance, this place where only heavy dark emotions, thoughts and feelings reside. Every now and then I would experience some sort of normality and, over the months, I slowly started to transform into this new reality which I had to relearn and accept. I appreciate that Matthew would not want me to grieve for eternity or to fall apart, just as you would not want your loved ones to either.

When my children were young, I was introduced to meditation, and this helped me to switch off, relax and connect to a deeper peace. It was during this time that I experienced a mystical / spiritual encounter. While practising an attitude of gratitude, which I had discovered through a meditation course, I connected to an energy which part of me instantly recognised but there is no easy way to explain it in words. This is the best I can do.

It was a moment where time was non-existent, as if time did not exist. It was a connection to an energy, but at the same time I didn't feel connected; I had an inner knowing that I was this energy. I AM this energy.

I recognised this energy from a time before I was born and something inside me knew I would be this energy when I'm done with this physical body, but at the same time, it was also in me in that moment.

I had an awareness that I was not really this physical body and that this world was just a tiny blip in our existence and in that moment, I knew I was this energy and I experienced my true magnificence.

I was completely at one with everything, but I don't know, or have the vocabulary to describe the experience. The words pure unconditional love does not do it justice. It was much deeper than anything I had ever experienced as a human, but I recognised it, it was who I truly was without this human entity and in that moment, I understood everything. My human understanding wants to call this energy - infinite consciousness.

This experience cultivated my belief that we are all infinite beings and that there is no death; although having this experience did not protect me from the grief I encountered when my son Matthew passed away. The human experience of grief cannot be side tracked, it has to be felt.

I work as a therapist and over the years many of my clients have come to me expressing the sadness of grief. By introducing them to the various techniques I use they were able to find peace and move on with their lives in a more positive way. Now it was my turn to use these techniques on me.

Through my experience I discovered that it is possible to have a different relationship with our loved ones who have died but while we concentrate on the loss and absence of them, we cannot know their presence. I have a deeper understanding now and I have realised that grief can be transforming; However, this book is not about reaching enlightenment through suffering!

My grief is about missing the physical presence of my son, the sound of his voice, his smile, his humour, his laughter, his hugs, his smell, his personality, him: Matthew.

It is still ongoing, but it feels lighter now and it's important you understand that. As a parent, I will never stop mourning my son and I will carry that with me as long as I live. There will never be a day when I will stop loving or thinking about him, but I have stopped mourning his physical death.

My grief is also for the life I had, and for the person I was before my son became ill and before he died. I am readjusting and settling into my new reality and it takes time to make peace with this new way of being. I am learning to love and accept the person I am now. My grief is mine and I write about it because it helps me. I hope this book helps you too.

Everybody has their unique way of experiencing grief, but it is not healthy to prolong the anguish for years. We can carry grief with us for as long as we like, or we can let go of it when we feel ready but if we never feel ready, that's okay too. When we do feel ready to move through it, we can enlist professional support and we don't have to do it alone. This book illustrates my personal journey and how I travelled through the process.

I have learned that grief is not a state on its own but a combination of different emotions such as, anger, sadness, disbelief, guilt, etc. Grief is not something to get over or release and although it is not a mental illness, it can quite easily become one. Grief is something to be incorporated into our lives and for me it feels like it will always be there, but I am growing around it.

I will feel my loss forever and I will always wonder, what would my son be doing now? Would he have had children? What would they be like? How would his career pan out? So many thoughts about how things would have turned out differently had he not died. Perhaps we don't tend to have the same thoughts about our elderly friends and relatives who die, but the death of a young person, that's not meant to happen!

This book has been written from my heart and my hope is that it will, in some small way, help others who are going through a similar journey.

I also hope this book will give some insight to people who are supporting others going through the grief experience.

This book will help people come to terms with their new identity and change in self after the death of a loved one. Maybe it will help them understand their new role in life or make them think about how their role has changed.

This book is for anyone seeking help in moving on, and hopefully, they will find practical advice and support within these pages.

This book is not only for people going through grief but also for people interested in self-development and for others who need to develop an empathy and understanding of grief.

I do hope people will find inspiration in this book and learn that life can be meaningful again after a loved one's death.

This book is for anyone who feels alone and broken after the death of a loved one.

You are not alone.

CONTENTS

INTRODUCTION

A few days after Matthew's death I remember getting in my car one night and just driving. I wanted to drive so fast, I wanted to hit something and instantly die. I felt so full of pain and deep, deep loss that I wanted to end my life. The only thing that stopped me from following through that night was the thought, *I might take someone else out with me by mistake.* Instead, I drove my car to the middle of nowhere and I screamed and cried and screamed and cried. It was the dead of night and there was no one around to hear me. I had never screamed and cried like this in my life and the sounds that came out of my body were like nothing I had ever heard before. I shook and trembled and screamed and cried some more. If anyone heard me from a distance, it would have sounded like a wounded wild animal. It is impossible to find the words to explain the incredible pain I felt and utter disbelief that Matthew was never coming home again. After a while I thought about my daughter and my husband and how could I not go on for them? They were hurting too. Matthew was made of tough stuff and he would be cross if I did not pull myself together. He used to say, *"Mum, if I can get through this, then so can you"*, and after a while I could almost hear his voice and see his face and see him holding up his clenched fist saying with determination, *"Come on*

Mum, you can get through this". Matthew saved me that night. Whether I imagined him there or not, he saved me.

I know I will get through it. I am learning to live and laugh and smile again because if I don't, I will be letting him down.

For clarity I should explain what happened.

At the age of twenty-five, and only three weeks into his new job as a News Editor for the Stratford Herald newspaper, Matthew was diagnosed with a very rare and very aggressive form of kidney cancer called, papillary renal cell carcinoma. He lived for just over two years from his diagnosis and during this time he touched and inspired many people.

As well as being a journalist he was also a talented musician and songwriter and he wrote a collection of songs which he recorded on his album *'Fightback'*. These songs were heavily influenced by his experience of illness.

He also wrote a blog which had over 50,000 hits and chronicled his journey with cancer.

We received many messages from people who have been touched by Matthew's journey. People explaining how his blog had changed their lives because he wrote with such positivity and insight.

Each time Matthew received more bad news about his illness he would allow himself time to process the information and then dust himself down and get back to being Mr Positivity. Writing about his journey really helped him and this is what prompted me to write, in the hope that it would help me too.

Writing these letters to Matthew has been like therapy for me. It helped me to get it out of my head and onto paper and I found the words just flowed. In fact, some days I couldn't type fast enough as I spilled out my inner thoughts and feelings. What I found really interesting and helpful was being able to read back what I had written. Reading the letters back to myself gave me a deep insight to what was really going on inside me. I looked at the specific words and sentences I used, and I noticed the tone in which I had written it. These were ideal topics to work on myself using the Emotional Freedom Techniques (EFT tapping therapy) and I became my own therapist. (There is more information about the Emotional Freedom Techniques (EFT) at the back of this book)

Over time, I realised that while I focused on the loss and absence of Matthew, I was missing the opportunity to notice his presence. Although I had accepted his death, writing to him felt like a continuation, as if I could still have a relationship with him. Writing to him created a space for this to happen.

Three months after Matthew died, I was standing at the kitchen sink peeling vegetables and I was thinking about the letters I had written to him since he had passed away when suddenly, out of the blue, I got an image of a book that appeared in my mind.

The title of the book was - *Letters to MATTHEW* - and *Matthew* was written in capital letters and in flowers, just like a funeral wreath. I knew that Matthew was there with me in that moment because I could sense his energy all around me. It felt like he was giving me a virtual hug and tears welled up in my eyes, but they were tears of love, joy and connection. In that moment, I knew he was with me, guiding me to write a book. I really believe he channelled the image to me, and he also knew how important it was for me to see his name in flowers.

I know Matthew's death has taken me on a deep and profound spiritual journey. Fortunately, I never got to a place where I lost my belief in a higher power, God, the universe,

Mother Earth, Source energy, Angels, or whatever you like to call it. I know there is more to life than this, but like everyone else, I don't have the answers, but I know there is something.

It would be easy to say there is no God after such an experience. But bad things happen in the world all the time; you just have to turn on the news. Why is it okay to believe in a higher power until something bad happens to you?

I realised that I did have choices.

I could cut myself off from the world and spiral into a deep, deep depression.

I could think, "*I'll deal with this stuff another time*" and keep myself busy using distractions like work, watching TV, etc.

I could decide that life is too precious and find ways to help me cope with my feelings, my emotions and my dark thoughts, and writing these letters certainly helped me.

Life is like a rollercoaster and I believe we came here for the ride. We came here to experience every emotion (positive and negative) and if we didn't have the lows, how could we appreciate the highs?

I didn't take any medication to deal with my sadness because I wanted to feel and experience everything that grief had in store for me. I'm not recommending this for others, but it was the right way for me. I chose to go cold turkey and meet grief head on and deal with whatever feelings, thoughts and emotions came up for me, but I had no idea how tough it would be. The contrast of my life before his illness and his physical death to my life now is vast and I am still learning to feel comfortable with my new reality.

I have intentionally not mentioned or named other people (including friends and family) as grief is a very personal experience and it would be unfair to include others.

I have mentioned my husband Bill, and my daughter Sarah, with their permission.

Sharing these very personal inner thoughts, emotions and details of life after Matthew's death is putting me outside my comfort zone. I am a very private person and opening up in this way is very challenging for me but if it helps just one person, I will be happy.

Perhaps this book will help other people understand and come to terms with their grief. Perhaps in some way a positive can come out of such a dreadful situation. What would be the point of going through such a dark time if you could not learn and grow throughout the process and use it to help other people?

You may think this book has been written too soon after Matthew's death, but initially, it was never meant to be a book. It was my own personal journal. Each letter to Matthew was written in real time and it captured everything I felt there and then and in that moment. Each post was written in true time while I was in the emotion, and it captured every little aspect of what I was feeling and experiencing.

If I had intentionally decided to write a book at a later date, maybe a couple of years after, or even ten years after his death, I would have lost the energy of that moment. I would have altered the memory with my recollection by adding, deleting or forgetting important information.

Initially it was only meant for my benefit to get those dark thoughts out of my head, but I soon realised how writing these letters were healing me, even transforming me and cultivating a new and different relationship with my son.

Some people may think I have shared too much information and that grief and loss is so personal it should be done behind closed doors. Some people think there is too much negativity out there already and who needs to read a misery memoir? I did ponder about how much to share with others but then I remembered one of Matthew's blog posts.

"I've always said these blogs would be an honest account of my situation. Whether it be good, bad or ugly, I've wanted to give the full story of what my life has been like since I was diagnosed with stage four kidney cancer." Matthew Bates

If Matthew could be open and honest about his situation then so could I, whether it be good, bad or ugly. Here is one of his blogs which helped me decide about going public regarding my experience with grief.

"I woke up to the news David Bowie had died of cancer at sixty-nine. For music fans everywhere, it will have been an extremely sad day, and I definitely felt it too – even if I must admit to not knowing much of his catalogue beyond the obvious stuff! But it wasn't his death itself that made me question certain things – it was the way he handled it.

That's because Bowie hadn't told anyone about his illness. He had kept quiet for eighteen months, released an album and then died quietly a few days later. It made me wonder whether that was the right way to go about it – apart from the death bit, obviously! But a few people on Twitter who I follow certainly thought so.

Firstly, it's important to say that I'm not the sort of the person who gets involved in the wave of emotion that finds its way onto social media when someone famous passes away. I understand why it happens, but I'm never too fond of the 'I'm grieving more than you' stuff that can go on. I'm also not a fan of the pretend grief that can happen when a celebrity passes away – not that it happened for Bowie, but it is the reason why some celebrities 'die' prematurely while others die more than once.

Having said all that, it was when I logged into social media and read some of the reactions to his death that I started to question my own decisions related to the cancer I have, and how I have handled it.

For instance, a former local radio presenter – who I have so much respect for from my time in Journalism – tweeted: 'Now that's dignity. Knowing and not telling. God Bless #Starman #DavidBowie.' *A colleague replied:* 'It's a dignity we'd aspire to, but rarely achieve.'

Another journalist, Coventry City fan and ex-Sky Sports presenter Richard Keys, said: 'What a wonderfully dignified exit David Bowie made. Never understood those who publicise their illness. Bowie was a genius and a gent. RIP.'

Both of these tweets had plenty of retweets and likes, meaning others agreed with their views. I searched for 'Bowie' and 'dignified' and found loads more with a similar outlook. The final straw came when a blog on the Spectator website was retweeted onto my homepage.

http://blogs.spectator.co.uk/2016/01/david-bowies-dignified-death-is-a-reminder-of-the-sanctity-of-private-life/

Its headline said - his 'dignified' death was a reminder of the sanctity of private life. *It claimed Bowie's silence was a 'Herculean' effort but also went on to criticise those who chose to go public.*

Here's a flavour of the article: 'Today, to be sick in private, to die in private, seems almost revolutionary. They say Bowie bucked trends (and in the process invented new ones) — well, he's just bucked one of the most powerful and nauseating trends of our era: the victim-therapeutic complex which demands that we keep nothing private, that we advertise our failures and fragile mortality to a watching, sadness-hungry world.'

Pretty strong stuff, then! All of it made me think to myself – was I right to tell people? Should I have 'kept my dignity' and stayed silent? I did just that for more than twelve months before letting out the news on Facebook but had spent a good portion of that silence trying to urge myself to go public.

I knew that old friends genuinely cared about my wellbeing, and I wanted people to have an explanation when they saw me in the street and wondered: 'God, Matt looks ill doesn't he!' I had reached the stage where cancer was affecting my everyday life too much for it to stay hidden any longer.

It took me a year to have what I thought was the courage to do it. A friend of mine has had cancer and hasn't told a soul about it. I've often thought of how brave they are – keeping news like that to themselves and getting on with daily life. Yet, when I went public, their first reaction was to tell me how brave I was."

Strange how we see things differently.

I know those who used the word 'dignified' did so in an innocent fashion, but I do wish people would take a step back sometimes and think about what they are writing. The problem is, of course, that it takes an event such as finding out you have cancer to realise how you can impact on others.

Before all this, I saw everything in such black and white. Every opinion came so easily. But I'm not so ignorant now, thankfully. I'm not always right, and not everything is black and white.

And I prefer it this way. It's one of the positives to come from this, I think, to have the ability to know what's important and take a step back in a situation before acting. To see things from other people's perspectives and know that everyone is fighting their own secret battle, and to not judge them without knowing all the facts.

I like to think it's having that attitude – and not the decision on whether to go public or not – that defines whether someone has dignity or not. To not just be worthy of honour or respect yourself – but to value, honour and respect the people around you, too.

I also think that I've learned one key lesson this week: don't go on Twitter so bloody much!"

Matthew Bates

Reading this particular blog post from Matthew's website made my decision to go public much easier. He blogged about his illness and his perspective of his cancer journey and he helped and inspired many people. He was always open and honest, and he wouldn't want me to be any other way.

We saw you getting tired and a cure was not to be, and an angel gently whispered, "Matthew come with me".

Friday, 15:05

Death – Shock - Panic - Chaos -
Disbelief - Confusion - Trauma - Overwhelmed - Sadness
Powerlessness - Hopelessness - Despair - Numbness -
Emptiness - Loss - Pain - Stillness - Spaced Out - Tears -
Sore Eyes - Weariness - Exhaustion

The following pages contain the heartfelt letters I wrote to Matthew after he died.

PART 1

LETTERS TO MATTHEW

Dear Matthew,

Leaving you behind was one of the hardest things I have ever done. I had to say goodbye for the last time and even though we knew this last goodbye was coming, in the end, it was still traumatic.

I stayed with you for hours holding your hand and touching your hair.

I am your Mum and I am supposed to protect you and keep you safe and I failed you.

I couldn't save you.

I placed a rose quartz crystal in one of your hands and a small teddy in the other. I sat with you for hours not wanting to leave but I knew you weren't there.

It was obvious - your life force – your soul – your consciousness – your existence – your being or whatever you like to call it was gone.

I remember thinking how your hair hadn't changed. It was still blonde and soft and it moved as I brushed it with my hand. I styled it with my fingers just how you liked it.

Your body was like an empty shell. A space suit. A body you didn't need any more. You had graduated, gone to Heaven or, as I believe, gone back to pure unconditional love energy, that same energy I experienced on a beach many years ago.

I knew you would be okay where you were, but I was still here, and I was not okay.

I was being forced to accept this new reality, a reality without you. It was a situation totally out of my control, and it felt so wrong, so unfair, so cruel, so uncomfortable and so, so sad. I had feelings I had never experienced before, and I do not have the terminology to explain them. There really are no words.

> *"I am not this hair, I am not this skin, I*
> *am the soul that lives within."*
> Rumi

Dear Matthew,

Each moment feels like a blur. I feel lost and empty and the disbelief is palpable. The pain inside is like a real physical pain and I can understand now how people can die of a broken heart.

My world is collapsing all around me and I don't know what to do with myself.

Life will never be the same again.

The postman brought a parcel from your university friends. It was a photo book of your time at university. What a lovely gift - but you are not here to receive it. I would like to ask a few questions as in some of the photos you look a bit worse for wear, but it did make us smile. We don't know much about your life at university, but we know you made some amazing friendships.

We've had a few visitors over the weekend with friends and family keeping an eye on us which was a good distraction because I did not know what to do with myself.

The pain is unbearable.

Dear Matthew,

We picked up your death certificate from the hospice today.

I just wanted to stay at home and hide under the duvet and not face anyone and it seemed cruel to be doing this so soon after your death.

The nurses said that the young Doctor helped prepare you after you died, and it was him that dressed you into your suit which is very unusual because it is not part of the Doctor's job description to do this. He had a soft spot for you and he wanted to do it. That really touched us to think that even in your death you received such special treatment. You always made such an amazing impression on everyone you met. The same Doctor handed us your death certificate today and we told him how much we appreciated everything he did for you. What a lovely man.

I wonder why they call it a death certificate. Normally a certificate is something you can be proud of and it should be framed and hung on a wall like your graduation certificate. A certificate is something to be celebrated; it has a positive connotation to it, but there's nothing positive about your death certificate. I suppose your death is like a graduation. You have graduated to the next level and one day we will graduate too. Perhaps it should be called a death graduation certificate.

The next job was registering your death and wow that was hard. You only died three days ago, and it was so painful to have to go into the town and face other people so soon. It seemed surreal being out in the world, passing other people living their lives, doing their thing, oblivious to our pain and loss.

The world was still spinning, and life carried on as normal for others but for me it seemed like I was in slow motion and I was on the periphery looking in. I felt as if we were living in this vortex of complete sadness and disbelief and that we were invisible but the only thing invisible to everyone else in town today was our emotions. People were too busy with their own lives to even notice us. What was going on for them? They were probably living in their own vortex of stress and we were oblivious to that too.

The lady in the registry office was very professional and she shook our hands. She didn't give me any eye contact and she didn't ask me any questions. Your Dad had all the paperwork and he communicated with her while I sat there with tears streaming down my cheeks.

My thoughts took me back to the time when we registered your birth and we were blissfully happy. We had the perfect family, a girl and a boy and our family was complete. Little did we know then that twenty-seven years later we would be doing this. Should I feel grateful that we had you for twenty-seven years because some parents do not have their children for that long? I didn't feel grateful in that moment.

How did we get to be here in this office, doing this formal, legal, cold hearted, form filling? It seemed so harsh and how did your Dad stay so focused? He has been amazing. He has gone into organising and sorting mode these last three days while I have collapsed into a withering wreck. You would be so proud of him. I was beginning to wonder why I was there in that office. I felt invisible and not needed but I did need to be there. I needed to witness this legal documentation being filled in and signed. As cold as it seemed, it was all part of the process of closure.

When everything was signed and sorted the lady shook your Dad's hand and then she grabbed both my hands and looked into my eyes for the first time. Suddenly a wave of emotion came over me as she explained how sorry she was for my loss, and then she explained that she also had a son called Matthew who was born two days before you and, in that moment, I knew why she hadn't looked me in the eyes earlier. In that moment, I felt her compassion and deep love, from one Mum to another, a deep connection which I will never forget. Perhaps you knew her son, perhaps you went to the same school or played football or golf together or perhaps you were just aware of each other. You knew so many people.

Then onto the funeral directors. The funeral director looked like Russell Brand. He was tall and dark, and he had similar facial features and mannerisms. Oh my God! Why would I think that at a time like this? Why is my mind having such crazy thoughts?

He was very professional, and matter of fact and we discussed what needed to be discussed in order to arrange your funeral. He asked us questions we weren't prepared for, but he said we didn't need to know the answer and that we could go away and think about things.

I wonder if they find it hard to do this job especially when it is for young people. I found myself zoning out and only hearing the conversation from a distance. I didn't like this feeling. I needed to be more present, but I couldn't take it all in and this was my way of coping with an awful situation. Your Dad was amazing once again.

We wanted everyone to be happy with the arrangements, but it was becoming obvious that there were going to be conflicting ideas and people were getting upset. It was taking all my energy to just survive and get through the day at this point and I couldn't cope with any other outside stresses.

Today was a tough day.

Dear Matthew,

Arranging your funeral seems surreal. You had talked about what you wanted and now here we were putting it into reality. No one should have that conversation with their child.

I remember you discussing the arrangements with me just after you were told you only had a short amount of time left. You had already made peace with your situation and you faced it with such grace and dignity. That should have made it easier in some way but there was nothing easy about it.

Arranging catering and ordering sandwiches is difficult when you have no idea how many people to expect. How could we arrange a funeral at such a difficult time?

Dear Matthew,

Emotions are high, and some relationships are at breaking point; how did this happen?

> *"Being the best you can be may never be enough, but be your best anyway."*

Dear Matthew,

You saved me today.
Were you really there or did I just imagine it?

Dear Matthew,

The postman brought more sympathy cards today; that's over 300 cards and letters now. He said, *"Christmas has come early in your house"* and I smiled and said thank you as I took the pile of cards off him.

If only he knew!

Dear Matthew,

I don't like it when people say. "You lost your battle with cancer".

Why do they think that is a good thing to say?

When people describe how cancer patients lose their battle, it makes me sad because it is an injustice to the people who die. The ones who live win, and the ones who die lose but you didn't lose. Each day you showed immense strength of character as you experienced everything that cancer brought into your life.

You definitely won.

You wrote about your experiences on your blog and inspired over 50,000 people. I hope you realise what an impact you made on the world with your positive energy.

You definitely won.

Everyone who met you, instantly warmed to you and you had an amazing capacity to connect to different people. This has been confirmed by all the cards, letters and messages we have received, and they are still coming. Some from people we had never even met.

You definitely won.

When people talk about cancer they use metaphors such as: *fighting a battle with cancer* or *winning the war on cancer,* but cancer is not the enemy, it is an illness. You never turned it into a battle and you were never a victim to cancer because you won in the game of life.

You definitely won.

Even though you were dealt such awful cards you were incredibly optimistic, courageous, strong, inspirational and hopeful throughout. And when the Doctor told you, you only had days left, I will never forget how you thanked the medical staff for everything they did. You had a calm energy about you, as if you knew, and you had already made peace with the news that your death was imminent. You always seemed to find a way through. You were amazing.

You definitely won.

You had cancer; cancer did not have you.

Your sister Sarah wrote a thought provoking blog about cancer today. I am so proud of her and how she is coping. She is incredibly strong, sensitive, empathetic, amazing, caring and loving and I am so proud of her.

I am so proud and honoured to be a Mum to two amazing human beings.

Sarah's Blog:

A LETTER TO MY BROTHER'S CANCER

For a long time before he died, and in the days that have followed his death, people have said "Fuck Cancer". It's a sign of solidarity. "Shit, I'm so sorry that happened. Fuck cancer."

If I'm honest, I have uttered the phrase myself.

Fuck you, cancer, for taking my brother.

But it's always said in anger towards you. It's said with an undercurrent of hatred. But if we look at what cancer actually is… It's a bunch of cells mutating and multiplying, just like any cell would do. Cancer doesn't know what it's doing is wrong. It's not evil, or thoughtless, or selfish. It doesn't know any better.

Saying "fuck cancer" is like saying "fuck you" to the seven year old bully who is frustrated and angry without a better outlet. The bully doesn't have any other way of expressing themselves other than to blow up. I'm not saying seven year olds are like cancer ("Hey Sarah, aren't you working on a childcare degree? I thought you liked kids!") *but I think, perhaps, we could deal with cancer like we would deal with the child bully. Don't punish or scold or act out in revenge... But open your arms, let them feel love and comfort, let them know that you are there for them. Let them know that there is another way to behave other than causing pain.*

Because when something causes you pain, send back love.

I thought maybe I should hate you, cancer. I thought I should be angry with you. But looking at what you are, seeing you as cells inside his body, I can instead see you as a part of him. You were trying your best to do whatever you were trying to do, and maybe you didn't know what you were doing was killing him. It's a very human thing to do, to keep growing and seeing how far you can push until the organism we are living on breaks. We've done it to our planet in the same way you did it to him. You were born from the cells of a man who literally fought until his dying breath, it's no wonder you fought back.

I forgive you, cancer.

When something causes you pain, send back love. Always, always, always... Send back love.

There's no way of knowing whether loving you, cancer, would have saved him. I doubt it. And now, cancer, you're gone too. You can't live without the body you were growing in. Your cells have died with him. Is anyone mourning you, cancer? Can I grieve for you? When you were alive, so was he. You would have had to leave him for him to survive, but up until two weeks ago you were both alive. Now you're both dead, and if I can't have him without you, I wish I could have you both back.

You might have killed him but you brought so many positive things into his life. The relationship between me and him got closer, to name one in a million things. How can you hate something that brought so much good?

So maybe loving you wouldn't have saved him... but I think it could help process the pain.

Send back love. Always, always, always.

Dear Matthew,

I'm feeling so lost and empty. My life has changed forever, and I still can't believe you will never come home again. I lay on your bed today surrounded by your things trying to make sense of everything.

I cried so much today and I wished this grief would just swallow me up and take me to a place where I couldn't feel any more. The pain is unbearable but there seems to be no other way to be.

How am I going to get through your funeral?

I found myself daydreaming and visualising your funeral in my mind. I had done this many times before but I used to stop myself and change the film role to a happy ending where you would go into remission and eventually be classed as cured. I can't do that now because your death has become a reality.

I know you are not in that coffin. I know you are in a place where time does not exist and only love counts. That same energy I experienced on the beach. This thought comforts me.

"If I can still breathe, I am doing well."

Dear Matthew,

I can't believe how lovely your funeral was.

Just writing those words do not make sense.

How can a funeral be lovely?

I do not remember leaving the house and getting into the funeral car, I just remember being in the car as it drove slowly to the church. I was worried about your Dad being sick in the car because he had felt physically sick in the bathroom just minutes before we left. He was thinking about having a brandy to settle his tummy but he decided against it in the end.

If you had seen us in the morning falling to pieces you would not believe we were the same people at the church. When we arrived at the church an immense sense of calm came over us. It was incredible. How did we go from complete wrecks to Mr and Mrs Calm in an instant?

There were so many people outside the church and so many people wanted to come up and hug us.

We were guided by the funeral people into position and we walked behind your coffin into the church. WOW so many people and so many young people, not something you see very often in churches today!

You could feel the love in the church and this helped us so much.

I held my head up high as I walked behind your coffin. I was so proud to be your Mum.

The entrance song we chose was recorded. (All Is Welcome Here by Deva Premal) Ideally, I would have preferred our musician friends to have performed this, but it would have been a big ask. I did wonder if playing this recorded song would be frowned upon by our many musical friends in the congregation and when the track started to jump, I thought, that's karma, it should have been performed live but hey ho! You were probably looking down thinking, *Oh my God, how embarrassing!*

I'm sorry I didn't cry at your funeral. I'm sitting here crying now as I write these words but there were no tears left for you at your funeral. It was as if I had used them all up and my bank of tears was empty. I need to replenish the tank.

The service was lovely, and your Dad was amazing.

You were easily embarrassed by your Dad but today Matthew you would have been so proud. His eulogy was perfect, and he delivered it perfectly and he got a round of applause. I like to think you were standing next to him giving him the strength to get through it.

Sarah was so brave as she stood at the pulpit and read out a prayer and I was so proud of her. How will she ever recover from her loss? To lose her only sibling, her little brother who shared a lifetime of experiences with her and the only other person who understands our family in a way that no one else could. Please watch over her Matthew.

The crematorium was full of your family and close friends and your best friend did you proud. He was such a good friend to you and his testimonial to you was emotional, funny and special.

Were you standing next to him? I like to think so.

We listened to a couple of your songs.

Friends sang – *You've Got a Friend.* (James Taylor version)

Another friend read out this poem, which means a lot to me.

Speak To Us of Children
And a woman who held a babe against her bosom said,

Speak to us of Children.
And he said:
Your children are not your children,
They are the sons and daughters of life's longing for itself.
They come through you but not from you,
And though they are with you yet they belong not to you.
You may give them your love but not your thoughts,
For they have their own thoughts.
You may house their bodies but not their soul,
For their soul's dwell in the house of tomorrow,
Which you cannot visit, not even in your dreams.
You may strive to be like them but seek not to make them like you.
For life goes not backward nor tarries with yesterday.
You are the bows from which your children as living arrows are sent forth.
The archer sees the mark upon the path of the infinite,
And He bends you with His might that His arrows may go swift and far.
Let your bending in the archer's hand be for gladness,
For even as He loves the arrow that flies,
So He loves also the bow that is stable.
Kahlil Gibran.

The Wake or, as we preferred to call it, *The Celebration of Your Life*, was at the Abbey where you played cricket. You would have loved to have been there! All your family and all your friends from way back were there. Your colleagues past and present and university friends too. We had a cricket style tea including cucumber sandwiches and cakes and scones.

We had arranged a display of your photographs from birth until you were an adult. You would have hated that, but we wanted to show you off. We wanted everyone to see what a fantastic son you have been over the years and we have been so proud of you.

We were completely washed out by the evening, but it had been such a very special day surrounded by all the people who knew and loved you.

I am so proud of your Dad and your sister and our family.

We will hold the memory of this day in our hearts forever.

Dear Matthew,

Now the funeral is over, it seems like life has to go on but there's nothing to focus on any more. There is this big empty hole which cannot be filled. Everyone else is getting on with living but life will never be the same again and I don't know what to do with myself. Your Dad has gone back to work and I am pottering around at home, but my thoughts are consumed with memories of you.

How did you get so ill?

Was it caused by an emotional trauma?

What could I have done differently as a Mum?

Should I have forced you to eat more fruit and vegetables when you were little?

Was it because I smoked when you were young?

Was it all those wine gums you used to eat?

Or, was it a soul contract arranged between us before we were born?

I keep tormenting myself with my thoughts.

"Falling down is part of life but getting back up is a choice."

Dear Matthew,

The house feels so different. It isn't a family home anymore and I think I want to move. Your Dad is being sensible and saying we shouldn't do anything for a few months and then we should see how we feel.

Everything looks dull.

Everything feels dull.

Am I depressed?

I don't think so, but I'm not sure.

Everything just seems dull, like there's no life in anything.

Your passing has sucked the life out of the house and all its contents.

Tears for Prayers

You know I feel your sorrow
You know I feel your pain
You fear that you have lost me
And we will never meet again.

Maybe you think prayers went unheard
Maybe you've lost your faith
But there is a bigger picture
And your Faith is what it takes.

"Those With Whom We've Walked
in Love, We Will See Again".
This is God's Divine promise
See, there really is no end.

Don't grieve for me for you must know
I'm in a bright new dimension.
Where beauty fills each joyous moment
Way beyond your comprehension.

So Rest in Peace Dear Loved One
Change your Tears to Prayers.
Know that everyone you say for me
Sends me Peace beyond compare.

For in Heaven time is nothing
You'll know one day for sure,
And there's nothing that will keep me
From holding you once more.

© Patricia Mary Finn - Divinerealisation.co.uk – Reprinted with permission

Dear Matthew,

We picked your ashes up today. I'm sure you weigh more now than you did when you were alive because they were bloody heavy. We placed your ashes on the coffee table and stared at them for a while. It was a surreal moment and I was surprised at how emotional I got. I know you are not in the ashes because you live in our hearts now, but I did get some comfort from bringing them home. We left your ashes on the coffee table for the evening while we watched the telly and when we went to bed we placed your ashes on your bed.

I might put them in the music room tomorrow for a while.

"The root of suffering is attachment."
Buddha

Dear Matthew,

It seems that every time your Dad and I sit down to chat we end up in tears. We don't mean to make each other cry but it is becoming clear that we both do this grief thing differently. I want to talk about stuff and he doesn't. His way of dealing with it is to keep himself busy, go to work, spend time in the music room, get friends in to record their songs, anything except sitting down and talking about his feelings. I'm a talker but I can't talk to just anyone, only certain people.

I've been doing a lot of tapping using EFT which helps, but there is no cure for missing you. I have been trying to practise mindfulness and living in the present moment, but the present moment is shit.

Here is a verse I used to share:

If you are anxious you are living in the future.
If you are depressed, you are living in the past.
If you are at peace you are living in the present.

I decided to re-write it:

My future is a new reality that has been forced upon me.
The past is no longer here except in my mind.
The present is shit because you're not here.

I've known your Dad for over forty years and we have gone through a lot of life challenges together, but this has to be the most difficult time. We still love each other very much and I know this deep love will get us through. It's important you know this.

> *"He will wipe every tear from their eyes. There will*
> *be no more death' or mourning or crying or pain,*
> *for the old order of things has passed away."*
> Revelation 21:4 – ESV

Dear Matthew,

I remember when you were first diagnosed; I became obsessed about finding a way to get you healthy. I was devoted to finding a way to support your recovery. I'm not sure what the difference is between being devoted or being controlling but I didn't care. All I wanted was for you to be well.

I became a Mum on a mission.

For over two years we both looked into every possible treatment or therapy or something that would help keep you here longer or better still, put you into remission and cure you.

The doctors are limited with their surgery, drugs and radiotherapy routes but there is so much more out there which we discovered.

Did we choose the wrong direction?

Perhaps we should have gone to that German clinic or Latvia where they offered you treatment.

What did we miss?

I know deep down we did the best we could, and I was always guided by you.

The adverts kept telling us:

The cure is just around the corner.

One day we will beat cancer. Help us make it sooner.

How would we feel if you had died the day before they found the cure!

We couldn't wait for science to come up with the cure, so

we started looking at a much more integrated way to support you, because you didn't have the luxury of time.

I spent hours researching, studying, reading books and gaining as much information as possible. I met some incredible people who had been written off by their doctors. Stage four terminal cancer patients who were cured or living with the disease like people live with diabetes. I made so many great connections to prove that it was possible and to put it on your radar that anything was possible.

You became open minded about alternative therapies and diet and supplements and anything that might help, and you did make many changes and I am so proud of you. Even though you were told the cancer was probably genetic, the tests were inconclusive, and I introduced you to the work of Bruce Lipton the Cell Biologist who explains that we are not victims of our genes.

You deserved to be that one in a million that goes into spontaneous remission. But it was not to be.

I miss our deep and meaningful conversations about life and death. I miss our conversations that sometimes went on until the small hours of the morning and I'm sorry if I became too much sometimes.

I remember one conversation in particular that made me feel really uncomfortable. We had just found out that a treatment you had been on had not worked and we were waiting to hear if anything else could be done.

You said, *"Mum I'm worried that you are not being realistic about my situation."*

I was always reassuring you that you would get better and that you would be a pioneer for your cancer type and that it was possible to get through this. I was always so positive, and I truly thought it was possible. I know I was annoyingly positive sometimes and I'm sorry.

That conversation was a difficult one. Hearing you talk about the possibility that you might die was unbearable. I wanted to fold you up into my arms and tell you everything was going to be okay but deep down I knew you were right. Another conversation that no parent should have with their child.

I remember your courage and your strength of character as you experienced everything that cancer brought into your life.

Death did not make you a failure or a loser, because as your body faded, your spirit flourished.

You definitely won.

> *"These past months have been the worst,*
> *but weirdly also the best, of my life."*
> Matthew Bates.

Dear Matthew,

I had a pizza and film night with the girls tonight and I laughed for the first time since you died, sorry! How can I laugh after such a short period of time? When is it appropriate to have fun without feeling guilty? I still miss you so much but, in that moment, I was pulled out of the grief and I felt happy. I know logically that it's okay to have these moments so why do I feel so bloody guilty?

Dear Matthew,

My life has changed so much since you've gone.

I don't miss making up your supplements each day, or your juices or your healthy meals, cooking everything from scratch, and making healthy soups.

I don't miss your hospital appointments and other appointments in between with your GP, blood tests, etc.

I don't miss that two hour round trip every other week up and down the motorway for your treatments.

I don't miss going shopping every other day for more fresh organic fruit and vegetables.

I don't miss the research and emails and telephone calls I did in the search for the cure.

I don't miss waiting in numerous waiting rooms constantly waiting to see various doctors and consultants.

I don't miss the panic and fear of what the next scan result will show.

I don't miss the anxiety of what a new day could bring.

I don't miss the long nights worrying about your future.

I don't miss the constant uncertainty.

I wake up in the morning now and think, what do I do today?

My routine has been turned upside down.

There's nothing to do any more.

So, I just potter around the house looking for jobs to do.

But I do miss doing those things because inside I am lost and, while I was doing all those things, you were still here.

Dear Matthew,

We are not eating properly at the moment and you would tell us off if you were here. We have gone from eating so well when you were around but it's different now.

How can we sit at the dining table and face your empty chair?

Tonight, we had salt and vinegar crisp sandwiches for dinner, in front of the TV.

I just can't be bothered.

"I can no longer see you with my eyes,
or touch you with my hands
but I will feel you in my heart forever." Author unknown

Dear Matthew,

Christmas is coming and it's everywhere; there's no escape. I'm not sure how we are going to get through this without you. You loved Christmas and you insisted on decorating the tree every year. When you were little I would re-decorate it after you and Sarah went to bed but the last few years you actually made a good job of it. I can't bear to put the tree up without you. I think we will go away this Christmas, somewhere hot but I better check with your sister Sarah first to make sure she's okay with it. She can come too if she wants.

Dear Matthew,

I saw someone I knew in the supermarket today. They looked at me then turned around and walked off. I stood there for a moment trying to make sense of it. Why did he do that? Was it too uncomfortable for him to say hi to me? Perhaps he didn't know what to say. I felt a jolt of sadness go through me and I realised that this was something I had to expect. Not everyone knows what to say and it is easier to avoid me than it is to talk to me and that's okay. How would I react? I hope I would react differently; maybe just hug that person and say, *"I'm sorry for your loss"* but maybe that's not appropriate in the middle of a supermarket.

What do you say to someone for the first time after a death, especially when you are in the middle of a supermarket? I stood there like a statue with people moving all around me oblivious to what had just happened. I wanted to chase him and say, *"Hi, how are you?"* Maybe if I had started the conversation, maybe I could have broken the ice, but the moment passed quickly, I needed to get what I went in for, get to the checkout and get out as quickly as possible without falling to pieces.

> *"If all you can do is crawl, start crawling."*
> Rumi

Dear Matthew,

I had my annual check-up at the hospital today: the same hospital where you had your surgeries and follow up consultations. I walked past your clinic and saw patients sitting in the chairs we used to sit in and I saw their faces. I wondered how long they'd been waiting. We always had to wait at least an hour each time and the anxiety of waiting to hear what the consultant had to say was always excruciating.

When I arrived at my clinic I thought I would have a long wait because that was our experience at this hospital, but I was called in after five minutes. That was quick!

The consultant is pleased with my progress and says he will see me again in another year. I was surprisingly relieved. I have seen so much cancer over the last two years that I think I have got an unconscious fear of getting it.

As I walked out of the hospital I passed the same patients sitting in the same chairs, still waiting.

I caught myself looking into the faces of everyone I passed on the way out and wondered, what's their story? Are they patients or visitors or maybe members of staff? Every face had a story. As I walked through the hospital corridors my mind went from one flashback to another. Remembering various times when you were a patient here. The conversations that delivered bad news. The surgeries and pain you suffered. The hospital blunders, the stress, the expensive car parking or not being able to find a car parking space. The memories flooded back one after another. My head was spinning.

It was a relief to walk out of the hospital into the fresh air, knowing that I have another year before I have to enter that place again, and suddenly I felt so guilty and so sad. You never experienced the feeling of getting good news. On top of that you usually had to wait an hour to see the consultant and then you were told bad news on top of more bad news. Your hospital visits here were always negative. I wish you had had this experience. I would have swapped places with you in an instant. I'm so sorry you never experienced this.

And here come the tears again.

> *"No one saves us but ourselves.*
> *No one can and no one may.*
> *We ourselves must walk the path."*
> Buddha

Dear Matthew,

We thought it would be nice to give your cousins a copy of your Kaleidoscope CD as a keepsake. We thought it would make a nice Christmas present for them.

Your Dad was in the process of sorting it out today when he discovered that you had updated the recording on the Mac so we decided to get a few more copies made of the updated version to give to family and friends.

He spent hours in the music room going through each track, re-mastering your updates. He said he felt very close to you during this time as if you were there sitting with him, guiding him.

Hope you don't mind but we made a different CD cover with various pictures of you on it. We added one of your quotes.

"I know I won't be around forever, but my music will be and that means a lot. It leaves something behind for my family to cherish." Matthew Bates

We are so lucky to have your songs to listen to and it gives us an enormous amount of comfort to hear your voice through your music. I hope our family and friends feel the same way.

Most importantly I hope you are happy with what we have done.

Dear Matthew,

Why do we have such strange dreams?

My dreams are usually about you and Sarah when you were both little.

Last night's dream was about your DNA.

A DNA expert was asking me if I had kept a lock of your hair because science had moved on so much they could now re-grow you in a test tube from the DNA of your hair. I said I didn't have a lock of your hair but I do still have your baby teeth. That'll do, he said, but I didn't know which baby teeth were yours and which ones were Sarah's. I keep both yours and Sarah's baby teeth in a pot in the bedroom but they are mixed up. There was no way of telling them apart and in my dream, I panicked in case we made another Sarah by mistake.

I didn't mean that in a bad way, Sarah!

Other dreams are that you are still alive and I wake up confused for a few minutes while I gather my thoughts.

I never used to remember all my dreams, but I do now. They are so vivid.

It's so hard.

Dear Matthew,

We set off for Lanzarote today to escape Christmas and it feels weird. It's our first holiday in nearly three years plus we've never been away at Christmas before. You loved to come on holiday with us and it seems odd to be at the airport without you. Getting on the plane was even weirder. I sat there and cried. The view out of the aeroplane window was beautiful but I couldn't see it properly because the tears would not stop flowing. It felt good to be getting away, but I felt conflicted because of the immense sadness I still held inside. The flight was good, and we soon reached Lanzarote and the hotel transport. The sun felt warm through the coach windows, but I found myself being emotional again. Oh, my goodness! Am I going to keep crying the whole week away? It's not looking good.

The hotel has an enormous Christmas tree and there are decorations everywhere. Christmas songs are playing and it seems like everyone is wearing a Christmas jumper. Have we arrived at the annual Christmas wearing jumper convention? I didn't put any Christmas attire in my suitcase. Doesn't look like we will escape Christmas after all.

Dear Matthew,

Christmas Day in Lanzarote and the sun is shining. I woke up to this note by my pillow.

Christmas Day 2016
No poem this year.
No present.
No words to describe how we feel.
No way we will ever forget.
But our love will always continue despite losing Matthew.

I am so proud of you Louise.
The way you conducted yourself over two years.
The love and devotion.
The fact you never gave up.

I love you so much for all this and everything.
Bill xx

Every Christmas and Birthday your Dad wrote me a poem in my card, as you know, but there were no cards this year. This was written on a page from a notebook and I will keep it forever.

Your Dad wants to go to church so we make our way there to find it is overflowing. No seats left in the church and the congregation has spilled out into the car park, so we decide to go for a coffee instead. Everywhere is open and it doesn't feel like Christmas in the town even though they have their fair share of Christmas decorations. It is far too warm to feel like Christmas. We went back to the church later to find it empty, so we went inside and sat for a while.

Why am I crying again? Stop it!

I wanted to light a candle for you, but it was not a wax candle, it was a digital candle. Technology had replaced the good old wax candle. What is the world coming to? Your Dad showed me how to use it. You put in a euro and an electric candle lights up. It doesn't feel the same as a proper candle, but the intention was there. I said a prayer for you too.

I sat in the hotel dining room this evening fighting back the tears. It's Christmas Day evening and I have just eaten the worst Christmas dinner ever. Normally at home we would be playing some board game by now or doing a family quiz which you would have spent weeks devising but here we are surrounded by strangers eating and celebrating. I missed Sarah too. Our first Christmas without her.

Most of the people are middle-aged couples like me and your Dad. I wondered what their stories where? How many of them had come here to escape Christmas?

Each dining table disconnected by a few feet and everyone doing their own thing. People not wanting to make eye contact with you in case you spoke to them. Perhaps they were carrying a deep sadness too and just wanted to survive the day.

I didn't feel much like socialising with anyone anyway. Perhaps I was putting up an invisible force field which repelled any kind of connection with anyone else other than your Dad.

I was communicating on an unconscious level saying, *warning, warning, keep away, unsociable lady, keep away!* Your Dad on the other hand was being annoying friendly and going out of his way to say *Merry Christmas* to everyone. He likes to make an entrance and he tried to make me laugh by doing a Norman Wisdom trip as he carried his five deserts back to the table. He had ice cream in one bowl, cake in another, fruit cocktail in another and an assortment of pastries and cream in the other two bowls. I remember thinking how embarrassed you would be if you were here now and that made me smile.

Christmas will never be the same again.

Dear Matthew,

It's been two months now since you died, and I miss you so much it is overwhelming. Even going in the sea today for a swim felt weird. You loved to be in the sea too. You got that from me. We would love to walk along the beach as a family looking for heart shaped pebbles and you would turn it into a competition to get the best one. Memories of our family holidays keep flooding my head but instead of making me feel good it just saddens me more. I am grateful for the many memories and I am grateful to have had you around for twenty-seven years because some parents don't get to keep their children that long, but the sadness continues.

"Most people are afraid of suffering. But suffering is a kind of mud to help the lotus flower of happiness grow. There can be no lotus flower without the mud."

From No Mud No Lotus (2014) by Thich Nhat Hanh with permission of Parallax Press, parallax.org.

Dear Matthew,

It's New Year's Eve and we've been home for a few days. We went to bed about 10pm because we felt sad and sleep would be an escape. I couldn't sleep, so I sat in your room for a while and I lit a candle. I thought about all your friends out celebrating and having fun. I remembered how much you enjoyed the New Year and how you always dressed so smart when you went out. It seemed cruel that you were no longer here. You should be out there celebrating, enjoying life, drinking and having fun. I cried myself into the New Year.

When the fireworks started, I knew we had entered 2017, a New Year, not the year you died in and I suddenly felt an overwhelming realisation that you died last year. Why is this upsetting me even more?

Last year, sounds so far away!

I felt so many emotions but mainly sadness, a deep, deep sadness.

"Having a rough day?
Put your hand on your heart and feel it.
That's life - so don't give up."

Dear Matthew,

I watched a cartoon today by Raymond Briggs, you know the man who made '*The Snowman*' and '*When the wind blows*' and it made me cry. The film is called, *Ethel and Ernest* and it is an animated film about his parents and their lives from the moment they met until they died. It was beautifully made and showed the ordinariness of their relationship and their time together, but the bit that made me cry was when they were having a street party to celebrate the end of the war.

Ernest saw a chap looking sad with his hands in his pockets and with his head hanging low and he approached him and invited him to come over and join the party. He asked him to come and have a drink and some fun, reminding him that the war was over, but the character just looked up to him and explained that his son had died in the war. Suddenly I completely connected to this sad cartoon character on the television and I felt his pain. I knew how he was feeling, and the tears ran down my face.

I feel like life is one big happy party and I am on the periphery unable to join the celebration. The world is still spinning, and people are living their lives, but my life is on pause. It is a strange place to be but being anywhere else would be even stranger.

I loved you so much and I still love you and I always will love you.

Nothing can change that.

"Stop beating yourself up.
You are a work in progress."

Dear Matthew,

Nobody seems to talk about you openly these days. When I mention you in conversation, a tumble weed moment happens.

One of your cousins shared something about you on Facebook today and it made me feel so warm and happy. Your Grandma mentions you, but most people try to avoid the awkwardness. People probably think it will upset me, so I'm sure their intentions are good, but it upsets me if they don't talk about you. Sarah and I talk about you all the time.

"We talk about you because you are still part of our lives."

Dear Matthew,

I saw someone you knew in the supermarket today and I panicked and changed direction. I can't believe I did that. I was ranting on before about how someone had done that to me and now I have done the same thing.

It was someone you knew really well from years ago, but I could not face talking to him. I walked to the back of the supermarket with my head down trying to frantically create what to say in my head just in case we did come face to face with each other. I don't think he saw me, but I can't be certain.

Each day seems to bring new challenges. They come out of the blue without warning, but I am not emotionally strong enough yet to deal with them.

I long for the ordinariness of my old life, but that's gone now. To be able to go to the supermarket without worrying about bumping into someone I know who's going to ask questions, or not ask questions.

How did food shopping get so tough?

Dear Matthew,

When you died, your Dad took on the role of informing people. (I don't know how he did that.)

He also kept an eye on your email in box just in case anyone slipped the net. Today you received an email from Victoria Derbyshire. She was replying to an email you had sent her and she obviously didn't know you had passed away. Here is her email:

Dear Matthew,

I'm writing to you because you sent me a very wonderful message when I was going through breast cancer treatment. It gave me such a lift and I want to thank you again for it.

I'm now writing a book about my diagnosis and treatment (www.facebook.com/DearCancerLoveVictoria/) and wanted to include some of the incredible messages I received from people - including potentially yours.

I was wondering if I do go ahead and include yours, you would allow me to mention your name please (either just your Christian name or both your first name and surname?). I am completely happy not to mention who it came from, though, if you would rather be anonymous.

I do hope you are well.
Kind regards
Victoria Derbyshire

I remember you mentioning that you had written to her which was typical of you always thinking of other people, but I didn't expect her to write back. Dad replied to her explaining that you had passed away and she sent back a lovely reply.

You touched so many people by being the person you are, and we are so proud of you.

Dear Matthew,

I need to start thinking about work again. The bills need to be paid and being self-employed means there's no compassionate leave or benefits of any kind. I'm not in a position to phone a boss and say, *I'm coming back to work next week,* so I have to build my business back up again. It's going to take time and energy and I don't have the same motivation any more. I haven't worked properly for months and I have lost my confidence. What if I've forgotten what to do?

Dear Matthew,

A funny thing happened in Ikea today. I went with your Dad and Sarah. We needed to get some bits and pieces and so we decided to stay and have some lunch while we were there. We all had the meatballs although I went for the vegetarian option and then we started looking for somewhere to sit. We couldn't find a place with four chairs because it was so busy. We hovered for a while looking for people who looked like they were nearly finished and then moved in. We eventually got a table by the window with four chairs. We settled ourselves down and started to tuck in when Sarah brought to our attention what had just happened. Why did we look for a table with four chairs when there are just three of us? There were plenty of places for three people. We all looked at each other trying to process what had just happened. We all did it, but it wasn't until Sarah pointed it out that we realised. I couldn't believe that we did that. We joked that you were here with us as you did like coming to Ikea.

Were you there with us?

Dear Matthew,

I had my first client today and it went well. As soon as I put my therapist head on, I was fine. It all came back to me; I haven't lost it and, for a while, I didn't think about you. I'm sure you would be okay with that.

Dear Matthew,

I did some work on my website today and I felt excited again. I remembered why I chose to do this work because it was my passion. I worked on a newsletter to send out to my clients inviting them to book a special offer. While I was focusing on this I wasn't thinking about you. I was still aware that I had a strange feeling in my solar plexus, but I carried on working on my website and newsletter. When I finished, I focused in on the strange feeling in my solar plexus and remembered it was a connection to the grief and sadness of losing you. Even though consciously I was engrossed in working on the computer, my body was still holding onto the emotion of loss. I know you would want me to carry on with my life and I am trying to do this, but it is so hard. Here come the tears again. I miss you so much.

> *"Your pain is the breaking of the shell that*
> *encloses your understanding."*
> Khalil Gibran

Dear Matthew,

I didn't cry today - yay!

This is the first day without tears since you passed away!

I still miss you loads and I want you to know that my tears are just love in liquid form.

Dear Matthew,

I thought I heard you knocking on the bedroom door in the night and it woke me up.

Was it a dream?

Occasionally, after you got ill, you would wake us up if you had an issue in the night and I would give you a reflexology treatment to settle you down again. There were times when you were distressed about a new symptom or maybe a new pain and we would reassure you but inside we were petrified too.

I suddenly remembered you were dead, and I must have dreamt the knocking on the door.

I lay there in bed remembering the various times when you knocked on the bedroom door. I can still hear your voice gently calling, "Mum…..Dad….are you awake?"

There were a few nights like this and I remember many nights waiting for you knock on the door and you never did because those nights you were fine.

I remember a time when I would lie there worrying about simple things in life like, waiting for you to come home after a night out. That seems like such a small worry compared to what cancer brought to our family.

"Don't give up, it won't always feel like this".

Dear Matthew,

A Facebook post popped up today which made me realise how much I've aged. It was a memory from three years ago. You and Sarah had brought me a bird table for the garden for my birthday and I was posing with it. It was still wrapped in gift paper, but it was obvious it was a bird table. My hair was different, and I didn't recognise the person in the picture. It looked like a different person, not me. It was a time in my life when everything was perfect. I had my perfect, happy, healthy family and my perfect life and I had no idea what was around the corner. That seems like a lifetime away now. I have more lines on my face and my hair has gone so grey. My outlook on life has changed and I feel like a totally different person to the one in this Facebook post.

Will I ever be that happy again?

"In the stillness, I am here"

Dear Matthew,

It was Mother's Day today and lots of people warned me that it would be a hard day. I was full of cold, so I felt pretty dreadful. Sarah brought me my favourite chocolates and gave me a beautiful handmade card which read:

To Mum
You are the best Mum in the whole world.
Everyone says that about their Mum
but everyone else is wrong!
Happy Mother's Day
Love you loads and loads and loads and I know Matt is
watching us and making sure you have a lovely day
Love from Sarah
Xxx

(The great thing about having a stinky cold is that people do not know when you are actually crying!)

We invited Grandma for lunch and we took her to a garden centre in the afternoon. I made sandwiches and scones for tea. It's the first time I've made scones since you died.

Dear Matthew,

I'm getting new client's book in and I am pleased about that and my business is starting to build up again.

A new client came today and she was telling me all about her children when she asked me if I had any children. I said yes, then paused. *"I have a daughter, who's thirty"* I said. My thoughts suddenly went into chaos.

Do I tell her about you? But then I would end up going into the story of what's happened. It was easier not to mention you.

Now I am feeling guilty because I didn't acknowledge you, like you never existed. Shit! What do I do in future? I need to think of a strategy in case I get asked that again. I'm sorry Matthew I didn't tell her about you. I want to tell the whole world about you. I feel like I've betrayed you. That was a weird moment of mind chaos but deep down I know you will understand.

> *"Sometimes we're tested - not to show our weaknesses but to discover our strengths."*

Dear Matthew,

Your Dad left me this note on the bedside table before he went to work today.

We are both doing this grief experience very differently, but this is proof that loves always shines through.

Louise, I love you sooooo much, never change (but you can if you want to) I will love you regardless.
Bill x

Dear Matthew,

Your cricket bat is still in the same place in the dining room. I visualise you occasionally picking it up and practising your swing just like you used to do. We'll never be able to move it. It's part of the furniture now. I'm still finding golf balls in the most unusual places and I'm sure you're playing games with me.

It's strange we never have any sport on the telly any more unless it's rugby. I was just getting into cricket too. Your Dad says, sport isn't the same any more.

Dear Matthew,

Coventry City went to Wembley today. You only missed it by four months. Some of your friends went and they asked your Dad to go with them, but he couldn't go without you.

Well the good news is Coventry won 1-0 against Oxford.

Miracles do happen!

Dear Matthew,

It's been four months now since you closed your eyes for the last time. I remember closing them for you. It was the last thing I could do for you as a mother. After twenty-seven years of being a Mum to you, especially the last two years supporting you through the difficult journey, it all ended there, in that moment.

My thoughts are still consumed by memories of you. I think about you all the time. When I wake up in the morning you are my first thought. I think about you all day and you are the last thought before I go to sleep at night and then I dream about you. A lot of my dreams are about you and Sarah. When I wake up in the middle of the night for a pee, I am still thinking about you. I miss you so much.

I don't think I ever want to stop missing you. Life without you is bad enough and what would it be like if I stopped missing you.

Dear Matthew,

I heard your Dad sobbing in the shower this morning, I mean really sobbing. I lay there in bed and listened, and the tears came out of my eyes without any thought process. I couldn't help him. He needed to have this moment, but it was hard to listen to. It was obvious we were a mess.

Nothing could take the pain away.

How long would we be like this for?

Do we need counselling?

Is this normal?

He says he's worried about me, but I'm worried about him.

Dear Matthew,

When people ask me, "*how are you doing?*" I can tell that most of them want me to say, "*okay thanks*" because they are almost nodding and smiling in advance, in the hope that's what I say. Before I have a chance to answer, there is a millisecond of awkwardness where you can sense their panic that I might break down or start telling them how I really feel and how bad my life is, so instead I lie and say, "I'm fine thank you".

Sometimes I say, "*okay thanks*" and smile and sometimes I say, "*oh I have good days and bad days*" and then smile. Sometimes I reply, "*as well as can be expected*" and some days I make a joke and say, "*well I haven't broken down yet today*" then I laugh and change the subject. You can see the relief on their faces that I answered correctly, and we can move on and talk about the everyday mundane things!

You develop an awareness of who really wants to know how you feel and who is just being polite. It takes a special person to really connect with you during this time. These people are empathetic, compassionate beings who genuinely care about how you are and they feel comfortable with your grief and really listen.

But how am I really doing and how do I measure how I'm doing?

It's impossible to measure the buckets of tears I cry or to quantify the pain in my heart that a paracetamol won't take away?

People ask me, "have you cried enough?" What sort of a question is that?

One person said, "it will hit you one day". What will hit me one day and will it be today or tomorrow or next year?

Hasn't it already hit me? What if it hasn't? How will I know if it's hit me?

It seems like everyone is an expert on grief and they are telling me what I should feel. Some people like to share what they went through when they lost someone or what their next door neighbour's brother went through.

Even though I have accepted your death, the waves of overwhelming disbelief that you will never ever come home again catch me without warning.

A thoughtful friend sent me these words in an email, and I managed to find the original author.

Grief is like a shipwreck:

As for grief, you'll find it comes in waves. When the ship is first wrecked, you're drowning, with wreckage all around you. Everything floating around you reminds you of the beauty and the magnificence of the ship that was and is no more. And all you can do is float. You find some piece of the wreckage and you hang on for a while. Maybe it's some physical thing. Maybe it's a happy memory or a photograph. Maybe it's a person who is also floating. For a while, all you can do is float. Stay alive.

In the beginning, the waves are 100 feet tall and crash over you without mercy. They come ten seconds apart and don't even give you time to catch your breath. All you can do is hang on and float. After a while, maybe weeks, maybe months, you'll find the waves are still 100 feet tall, but they come further apart. When they come, they still crash all over you and wipe you out. But in between, you can breathe, you can function.

You never know what's going to trigger the grief. It might be a song, a picture, a street intersection, the smell of a cup of coffee. It can be just about anything...and the wave comes crashing. But in between waves, there is life.

Somewhere down the line, and it's different for everybody, you find that the waves are only eighty feet tall. Or fifty feet tall. And while they still come, they come further apart. You can see them coming. An anniversary, a birthday, or Christmas, or landing at O'Hare. You can see it coming, for the most part, and prepare yourself. And when it washes over you, you know that somehow you will, again, come out the other side. Soaking wet, sputtering, still hanging on to some tiny piece of the wreckage, but you'll come out.

Take it from an old guy. The waves never stop coming, and somehow you don't really want them to. But you learn that you'll survive them. And other waves will come. And you'll survive them too. If you're lucky, you'll have lots of scars from lots of loves. And lots of shipwrecks.

© G. Snow via Reddit.com circa 2012. Reprinted with permission.

These words resonate with me so much. Yes, the waves are getting slightly smaller and yes there is space between the waves now but occasionally a tsunami comes along without warning and I am back to square one once again.

Dear Matthew,

I still feel overwhelmed with the negative memories I carry of your journey through illness and pain.

I remember times when you were treated by doctors and consultants with no bedside manner or compassion. All I can think of is the negative experiences you went through: the hospital appointments, the unexpected appointments with infections or a new symptom; the endless sitting around hospital waiting rooms, the scans, waiting for the scan results, blood tests, ambulances.

We learned new words like, '*scanxiety*'!

How can life ever be the same again?

The negative language in which the medical professionals used and the tone in which they delivered any bad news, some matter of fact and others with compassion, such a contrast.

The medical professionals are used to dealing with people who are ill, but I often wonder, how would they like there child or relative to be spoken to?

The whole experience of over two years of stress and anxiety and watching you, the person I brought into this world and loved and cherished for twenty-seven years slip away. They spoke of no hope, there's nothing else, no treatments etc, etc, etc and when you constantly hear that, what message does it send to the unconscious mind? Did you take all this negative medical language onboard? I know you cultivated an open mind after a while, but how many of their negative words did you believe? Being told there is no hope from these influential people has the potential to create and rewire a negative neural pathway in the mind sending doom and gloom information into every cell in the body. This is called the nocebo effect. For example, if a well behaved patient is told he only has six months to live and he believes it, he will die on cue. Is this what happened to you? Their words carry so much power. If only they knew!

I'm getting fed up with the adverts on the TV about cancer too. They keep telling us they are winning the war on cancer but why do they need to turn it into a war and if they are winning why are more and more people getting it. I remember a time when we were being told that one in sixty people would get cancer but now it's one in every two people. That's not winning!

And those bloody Macmillan coffee and cake mornings! Let's eat loads of cake, full of sugar (very healthy) and help beat cancer together. It's like saying, *"Let's have a cigarette party and raise money for lung cancer"*.

Oh, and let's run around a park wearing pink for cancer. It is great to see people outdoors exercising and these people have great intentions but where does the money go? Does anyone actually know? People get sucked into thinking they are helping cancer patients but who gets the money? It's probably paying for those expensive adverts on the TV or the big executive wages.

I may sound resentful, but with all the millions of pounds raised, and all the research done, wouldn't you think fewer people would be getting it by now? I don't believe they are winning their so-called war on cancer because all the money in the world is not going to cure cancer.

We need to start eating more natural foods which contain the essential nutrients and minerals that our bodies are designed to process. We need to start eating a more plant based diet, without sugar and unhealthy processed food and we need to start drinking more clean water and cut down on fizzy drinks and alcohol. We learned about all of this too late to save you unfortunately, but we were getting there. We just ran out of time!

We learned a lot along the way, but it is information we should have known about all along. Would it have prevented your cancer, we will never know?

They seemed to think your cancer was genetic but in this new world of epigenetics, the theory is that our brains' neural pathways are really running the show. Our mindset helps to build these neural pathways and they have the ability to turn on and off specific genes. Neuroplasticity is flexible, and we can influence how this works just by our repetitive thought patterns. We are not victims to our genes.

Sorry, I am getting on my soap box here and you are probably getting annoyed with me. The light is flickering on my desk so that means you are probably laughing at me or you don't like me writing about this kind of stuff. I can almost hear you saying, *"For God's sake Mum, You're not a bloody neuroscientist"*.

Maybe you are just not happy with my grammar and writing style.

I'm not a bloody writer you know!

It's good to get stuff off my chest.

I haven't changed much, have I?

I'm still nuts!

I'll shut up now!

> *"The soul is the same in all living creatures,*
> *although the body of each is different."*
> Hippocrates

Dear Matthew,

A client came for a treatment today who hadn't been for a while and, on leaving, he said, *"oh, by the way, how's your son doing now"*?

Well, that was awkward!

I had to explain that you had passed away.

Obviously, he was horrified and embarrassed and God knows what else and then I needed to rescue him.

"It's okay" I said. "You weren't to know, don't worry". I reassured him that he hadn't upset me and he went on his way. I shut the door behind him, came into the living room, expecting to burst into tears.

Nothing, no emotion.......I must be getting good at this grief thing!

This could potentially happen again, but I was pleased with how I coped with it.

Dear Matthew,

They played *Trouble* by *Coldplay* on the radio today. I was just parking behind the bank when it came on. It's amazing how music can have such an effect on our emotions. I sat in the car with tears streaming down my face. I remember when you used to play this on the piano. You were about thirteen or fourteen years old and you sang it so well and you even performed it at one of our barbeques. You were so shy back then that most of your friends had no idea how talented you were.

> *"Sadness is but a wall between two gardens."*
> Kahlil Gibran

Dear Matthew,

I went to a funeral today. It was for the husband of a friend of mine. Oh, my goodness, I cried so much! How did I not cry at your funeral but cry so much for someone else I never really knew?

He was a granddad, a father and a husband and I connected to the sadness felt by his family. I knew how raw their emotions were, it was palpable. The hymns and prayers and testimonials were all triggers for me and being in a church again surrounded by so much grief was overwhelming.

I said a prayer for you too.

Grief
I had my own notion of grief.
I thought it was a sad time that followed the death of someone you love.
And you had to push through it.
To get to the other side.
There is no pushing through.
But rather, there is absorption.
Adjustment. Acceptance.
And grief is not something that you complete,
but rather you endure.
Grief is not a task to finish and move on,
but an element of yourself, an alteration of your being.
A new way of seeing.
A new definition of self.
© Gwen Flowers – Printed with permission

Dear Matthew,

We never close your bedroom door, you know. The only time it used to be shut was when you were in your room. We used to use this as a gauge as to whether you were at home or not. If the door was shut, especially if you had been out late at night we knew that you were home safely tucked up in bed.

I just had a fleeting thought that if I closed your door, I could pretend you were in your room, just like old times. It was just a thought though and I ignored it!

It's amazing how much dust collects even though your room is empty.

Dear Matthew,

I started working on my gratitude journal again today which is part of the home study course I am doing. I had put the course on hold while you were poorly but I'm getting back into it again now.

The gratitude journal is really helping me. I am collecting quotes, verses and pictures that make me happy and I am putting them into a book. It's a healthy project to do because while I am focusing on collecting positive quotes, verses and pictures that make me happy, I actually feel happy too.

It will be a good resource to go to when I am struggling.

"Holding onto grief hurts - moving
on hurts - letting go hurts -
I will endure sadness for it opens my soul."

My soul must have a bloody gaping big hole in it now!

Dear Matthew,

It's Easter Sunday today and I'm okay. I thought I would struggle but it was just another day without you.

Your Dad and I went out for a 5k run this morning. It was your Dad's first 5k and he did great. He was faster than me which was annoying, but you would be so happy to know he has started running.

Sarah came for dinner and we watched the film *Mamma Mia* this afternoon and just chilled out. Even though we did eat far too much chocolate it didn't feel like Easter Sunday. Probably because you weren't here.

"Don't give up, it won't always feel like this".

Dear Matthew,

I have been doing a lot more tapping (EFT) recently and it is helping me enormously. I am aware of some resistance to letting go completely because although it hurts holding onto it, it also hurts to let it go. I can't bloody win!

I can't just stop grieving you overnight.

I don't want to stop grieving you at the moment.

I feel there needs to be a healthy timescale that is acceptable to me.

I am also scared that if I did clear all my emotional baggage over this grief that it would make me into a robot, devoid of any sensations.

I came here to experience this stuff so damn it, I will experience it and only I will know when it is time to say okay, enough is enough. I am in control of how I want to do this grief thing and I am pretty good at doing it. I am becoming an expert at grieving.

Dear Matthew,

Today I am getting a sense that it is getting easier.

I am functioning quite well as I am at the moment.

I am finding life is okay in between the waves and the waves are coming less often and they are not so big.

I am able to sit and watch a TV programme and not think about you constantly.

I am able to have a conversation with a friend and for a while forget my grief.

I am able to take on clients and get a sense of that passion that I once had for my work.

I am able to get through most days without crying.

I am spending less time pottering about in your bedroom.

The tapping has helped me so much and I realised today just how far I have come.

Dear Matthew,

Oh dear! I spoke too soon.
I am a mess today.
Where did that come from?
I just miss you soooo much, it's overwhelming.

> *"Life is - laughter and tears, delight
> and defeat, joy and sorrow."*

Dear Matthew,

There is a tiny robin that comes onto the patio every day and looks through the window. We have staring competitions and I usually win because he or she is very jittery, and it flies off at the slightest thing, but it isn't long before it comes back. I had the urge to look up the spiritual meaning of a robin today because I felt it was trying to tell me something and I couldn't believe what I read:

When a robin redbreast constantly visits you or crosses your path, a loved one in heaven is saying, 'hello! I'm with you!

Well, that made my day. Thank you, Mr Robin. I hope the neighbour's cat doesn't catch you!

Dear Matthew,

It's my birthday today and I thought it would be just another day without you, but the tears started last night when I went to bed. I was full of sadness and I missed you so much. I had a bad night and I felt knackered when I woke up this morning. I dragged myself into the shower and went through the usual morning routine, but I couldn't shake off that feeling of deep, deep sadness.

I lay on your bed for a while and chatted to you out loud. Did you hear me?

I know you are fine where you are. I know you are in a place of pure unconditional love. I take comfort from knowing you are okay.

I am not okay today.

I won't be getting a card from you and I won't be seeing your smiling face or get a birthday hug.

I listened to your album kaleidoscope this morning and it was good to hear your voice. We are so blessed to have your music to listen to. You live on in your music and in our hearts.

I met Sarah for lunch and we went to Stratford for the afternoon.

She said she could feel your presence when she wrote out my birthday card. She said she felt the same thing when she wrote out my Mother's Day card too, but she was too scared to tell me in case it upset me. I was driving as she was telling me this and the tears streamed down my face and I nearly crashed the car, but they were tears of joy because your sister felt your presence. That made my day. That was the best birthday present I could ever get.

We had a lovely lunch and afternoon and I always

feel uplifted in Sarah's company. We have such a strong connection and we have great conversations and we always talk about you.

I went out for a meal with your Dad in the evening and we had a delicious lasagne. I could see your Dad was struggling. He doesn't like to talk about his feelings much.

That is my first birthday without you, done and dusted!

Dear Matthew,

I am still cooking too much food at dinner time and I hate wasting food, so we end up eating it all and then we wonder why we put on weight, but at least we are eating better these days.

We didn't have an appetite for a long time after you died, and we lived off crisp sandwiches, toast, chocolate or sometimes we just missed meal times completely.

Now we are eating healthier and working towards improving our eating habits. I wish I could remember there are just two of us to feed because I keep making enough for three.

Why am I still doing this?

We haven't sat at the dining room table since you left. We couldn't bear to see your empty place.

One day we will, but not yet. We will continue to be slobs and eat off a tray in front of the TV.

The TV is such a good distraction.

"Peace comes from within. Do not seek it without."
Buddha

Dear Matthew,

I hope you don't mind but we wear your clothes sometimes. Your T-shirts and jackets fit me perfectly and I'm sure when I wear your running shirts, I run faster.

Your Dad likes wearing your ties for work. I didn't realise how many ties you had, and they do suit him. Much better than those old man ties he used to wear.

We gave a lot of your clothes away to your young cousins. You always liked to pass your clothes onto one cousin in particular but he wouldn't fit into any of them since he shot up. I think he sleeps in a grow bag because he is so tall. I'm pleased your clothes have gone to family as it doesn't feel like we are getting rid of them. You would have passed them onto your cousins eventually anyway.

You still have a wardrobe full of clothes and so many shoes you could give Imelda Marcos a run for her money.

Clearing out your stuff completely is so very difficult, and I don't how I will feel when it has all gone. I am only doing it slowly, a bit at a time. I don't want to look at empty wardrobes and shelves because that makes it even more real.

All your university work is still in boxes collecting dust. How can we just throw it out? All that hard work.

You have so many good quality books which I could take to the charity book shop but what do I do with your bits and pieces. Things you collected over the years like golf memorabilia for example, I wish I knew what to do with it.

Each time something else goes, something inside hurts.

"You only lose what you cling to."
Buddha

Dear Matthew,

A few years ago, I went to a talk by Dr David Hamilton. I remember him talking about how we can influence our emotions by learning clever little tricks. One of the tricks is to smile even when you feel sad. When you smile, tiny muscles around the lips and face tell your brain that you are smiling, and this releases endorphins, the feel good happy chemicals.

I'm open to anything, so I looked in the mirror and smiled at myself, but I just felt stupid.

I practised my smiling technique as I went along with my morning routine. I smiled as I cleaned the bathroom and I smiled as I cleaned the kitchen and I smiled as I prepared my treatment room for my first client of the day. I smiled so much my face ached.

I must admit it did help a bit. After the initial stupid feeling I did get a shift and it did help to make me feel better.

It is a constant uphill struggle though to keep myself moving forward in a positive way. It used to be my natural default to be optimistic and upbeat and I was a big fan of the Law of Attraction. I had my vision board, my gratitude journal and I remember a time when I was manifesting great things in my life. I used to say, *"How much better can it get?"* but those days are gone. How did I manifest all this crap!

I know I won't always feel like this.

I have to remind myself that I came here for the ride.

I came here to experience all these emotions and sometimes life throws things at you that are out of your control. That's life!

Sometimes I see myself from another viewpoint, my higher self. I can observe the person who is Louise Bates and see things from a different perspective. I can see what an amazing person I am and how well I am coping. I forget to do this sometimes because I allow myself to get sucked into all the grief and sadness trance.

I will continue to do what I am doing, and time will be my healer.

Yes, I will use EFT and I will practise my smiling and I will work on my gratitude journal and I will feel what I feel and allow myself to feel it. I will be gentle with myself and I will work through this process and I will do it for me, but I will do it for you too.

Writing these letters is definitely helping me too. When I read them back to myself I get a deeper insight into what's going on inside. It is the perfect way to record my thoughts and feelings and it also helps me to maintain a relationship with you. Sometimes I talk to you out loud too, can you hear me?

Blessed are those who mourn, for they shall be comforted"
(Matthew 5:4) KJV. The Lord will wrap His arms of
love and comfort around those who trust in Him.

Dear Matthew,

I haven't seen the little robin since I looked up its meaning. I hope the neighbour's cat hasn't had it. Perhaps he knew I got the message and he has been sent to someone else.

The garden is looking lovely and the hedgehogs are coming to the feeding station every night. The birds are flocking to the bird table and we can feel summer in the air, but it doesn't feel the same without you.

I miss the energy you brought into the house and garden. I miss hearing the sound of your cricket bat as you practised hitting cricket balls and I miss the divots in the lawn after you practised your golf swings. I miss you cutting the grass and trying to get the perfect cricket wicket in the lawn.

I'm still finding cricket balls, tennis balls and golf balls in the flower beds and I never want to stop finding them.

Dear Matthew,

Some days I am able to be okay but then it visits me in my sleep and it crashes into my dreams. It wakes me up and prevents me from going back to sleep. It sucks my energy and demands my attention. It crowds my heart and tries to steal my peace and today I feel broken.

Well done grief, I am well and truly knackered today.

Dear Matthew,

It was your six month anniversary today Matt; wow, six months since you died.

I've survived six months without you; surely it will start getting easier now.

I found myself constantly looking at the clock thinking about your last day and reliving every minute.

I spent your last night by your bedside talking and dozing and talking and dozing. We had said everything we needed to say previously but it was a special time which I will be forever grateful for. We held hands and chatted. I gave you a reflexology treatment to help you settle and later I gave you reiki while you slept.

I remember being so tired from lack of sleep and my eyes were sore from all the crying.

I waited for you to go into a deep sleep and then I settled into the chair next to your bed. I covered myself with a blanket and prayed you would have a good night. I asked the angels to heal you and leave you here. I pleaded with God not to take you.

A few years ago, I read a book called 'Dying to be me' by Anita Moorjani. She had been ill with cancer for almost four years. Over time her body became overwhelmed by malignant cells which spread throughout her system. As her organs failed, she encountered a near death experience which she writes about in her book. She eventually made a full recovery and now she does talks all over the world sharing the story of her near-death experience.

I begged the powers that be for you to have this experience too. I was praying you would make a full recovery, just like Anita. You could also write books and travel the world and share your story. Your background and experience as a journalist and editor qualified you for the job. Your expertise with social media and your personality would be the perfect fit. You could reach thousands of people through your blog, Facebook and Twitter. You would make a great PR man for the God cause, but God missed a trick there!

They obviously had other plans for you.

As I rested in the chair with my eyes closed, I savoured every moment I had left with you. While you were asleep I could hear you breathing and I knew you were still with me.

I was wondering if any angels were hovering in the room waiting for the moment to whisk your spirit away.

The room had a very serene energy to it and there seemed to be a great sense of calm, or perhaps I was feeling numb.

I was just drifting off to sleep when I heard you call me "*Mum*".

I jumped up and said calmly, "*yes, what is it?*"

You said, "*can you do me a favour?*" and of course I said "*yes, anything*".

There was a pause for a moment and then you asked, "*can you stay awake, and don't let me go?*"

I can still hear your voice saying those words as I type this letter to you.

Those words gave me such a massive emotional charge. (And still do)

I don't know where I got the strength to stop the tsunami of tears inside. I wanted to be strong for you and I managed to control the surge that engulfed my body. It was like a tidal wave of mixed emotions including a deep, deep love and strong protection that every parent feels for their child and a feeling of helplessness and hopelessness and disbelief that this was real. How I managed to contain myself, I'll never know. Here you were this grown-up child of mine, at the age of twenty-seven, but you felt like my little boy.

In that moment, you were my new born baby, the one year old, the toddler, the primary school child in your smart school uniform, the teenager, footballer, golfer, cricketer, musician, university student, the journalist. In that moment, I saw your life flash before me and I experienced all the joy you brought to me in an instant. I wanted to wrap you up in my arms and squeeze you so tight and tell you everything was going to be okay. The situation of you being in the hospice was out of my control but how could I ever let you go? And yes, I stayed awake all night watching you breathe, reassuring you every now again and surrounding you with the love only mothers know.

It was a long night but not long enough for me.

Every now and again you would wake up and ask if the day had begun. A strange thing to ask but you were desperate for the day to begin. When the sun started to rise, I opened the curtains and welcomed the day in, your last day, your last sunrise.

Your room looked out onto the hospice garden and we could hear the birds singing. The world was still spinning and life outside the hospice had some sort of normality to it. I imagined other people getting up as normal and going about their normal day. It was Friday and people would be looking forward to the weekend. Other people had plans, a future, but you only had hours left.

The nurses were like angels the way they glided in and out of your room and the care they gave you that night was incredible. They showed so much love and compassion to a level I have never experienced in my life before. These human beings were something else. They cared for me as much as they cared for you too and their hugs were incredible.

I remember one of the nurses sitting with us for about an hour asking questions about you. She wanted to know what you were like as a baby and I told her how good you were and how contented and easy to look after. She wanted to know what you were like at school, "*were you a naughty boy?*" she asked smiling. I told her you were never naughty at school and I told her how parents' evenings were always a pleasure. She asked lots of questions and every now and again you piped up with a funny comment, so we knew you were listening even though your eyes were closed. This nurse was very generous with her time and I will always remember how she made such a difficult time very special for us. There truly are earth angels on this planet!

As the day broke more visitors arrived and you drifted in and out of sleep.

When you did take your last breath, I wasn't holding you. We were waiting for the nurses to rearrange your pillows and I was sitting on the arm of the chair at the end of your bed. I turned away for a second and when I looked back you were gone.

Just like that!

Gone!

I wasn't holding your hand and I wasn't present with you in that moment when you took your last breath. I'd promised to not let you go and the moment my mind got distracted by all the commotion of nurses coming and going, you disappeared.

Where you waiting for that moment?

Was it hard for you to let go too?

Perhaps you took that moment to slip away or perhaps it was just bad timing.

It wasn't supposed to happen like that.

I had held onto you all through the night, all morning

and only taking quick loo breaks, worried in case I missed that moment.

I wanted to be holding your hand and be present with you when you took your last breath.

If I had been holding your hand while you passed over, it would have felt like I had handed you over.

I was there when you came into the world and I must take comfort that at least I was in the room when you left, even if we weren't holding hands.

I keep beating myself up because I didn't have any physical contact with you as you took your last breath.

I shouldn't have let you go.

I want you to know I will never let you go.

I know you have returned to infinite consciousness now, but you are also in my heart and the hearts of all the people who love you.

Fly high with angels and thank you for being in my life for twenty-seven years.

Death is nothing at all.
I have only slipped away to the next room.
I am I and you are you.
Whatever we were to each other,
That, we still are.

Call me by my old familiar name.
Speak to me in the easy way
which you always used.
Put no difference into your tone.
Wear no forced air of solemnity or sorrow.

Laugh as we always laughed
at the little jokes we enjoyed together.

Play, smile, think of me. Pray for me.
Let my name be ever the household word
that it always was.
Let it be spoken without effect.
Without the trace of a shadow on it.

Life means all that it ever meant.
It is the same that it ever was.
There is absolute unbroken continuity.
Why should I be out of mind
because I am out of sight?

I am but waiting for you.
For an interval.
Somewhere. Very near.
Just around the corner.

All is well.

Nothing is past; nothing is lost.
One brief moment and all will be as it was before only
better,
infinitely happier and forever we will all be one together
with Christ.

Henry Scott Holland

Dear Matthew,

Your Dad is racked with guilt saying he should have been around more during your illness. He believed everything was going in the right direction because we were doing so many alternative and complementary therapies and finding out all the different ways to support you. We all believed you were going to make it.

I spent more time with you because I worked from home and it was easy for me to take time off to support you. Being self-employed made it easy to take time off, but I didn't get paid when I took time off. Your Dad has always been the main breadwinner, so it made sense that he carried on working.

He still feels so guilty about it now and nothing I say helps him.

Dear Matthew,

I realise now just how far I have come in six months because the intensity of the grief feels less strong. Thinking back to what I was like six months ago, I can see the contrast. Becoming aware of this makes me feel quite conflicted because surely it is too soon to feel okay about you not being around anymore.

Please do not think this is an indication or gauge to measure how much I loved you and still love you.

I am sure you will be proud of me. You wouldn't want me to be falling to pieces six months on. You wouldn't want any of us to fall to pieces, I know that.

Your Dad is struggling. He sees me doing all this tapping work using EFT and he sees how far I have come and he said to me the other day, "you're leaving me behind".

We had a long chat about how we are both dealing with this differently. Your Dad is doing it the long and painful way, but I mustn't compare the different routes we take. I will never leave him behind and I will always be there for him encouraging him to talk and share his feelings and I will be guided by him. Whatever speed he wants to go, that will be right for him and I will be there, and I know you will be there too.

Dear Matthew,

We did another 5K run this morning and I visualised you running with us. I wore one of your running shirts which I'm sure helped me.

You were running in front of me, but you were running backwards facing me and spurring me on saying, "Come on Mum, you can do this, keep going, you're doing great" and then you turned around and ran ahead to catch your Dad up shouting encouragement at him too. Then you returned to me telling me how well I was doing.

I remembered how physically fit you used to be before your diagnosis and surgery and how hard you tried to get back to full fitness. It doesn't seem fair that someone so physically fit and young should die of cancer. You never smoked and although you had your occasional drunken nights out like others your age, you were never really a drinker. Life is unfair sometimes.

I wonder if you are playing sport where you are now. All the famous sportsmen and women who died before you and you could be up there with the best having the time of your life. I truly hope so.

I visualised you well and healthy and smiling as you ran with me today.

Did I really imagine it or were you really there?

Dear Matthew,

You would be really interested with what's happening at the moment. It's the local elections. I wonder who you would have voted for this time around?

I miss listening to your conversations with your Dad about politics. The debates you had together were fascinating and you knew and understood this topic much better than me. I used to listen to you and it influenced how I used to vote because you were so knowledgeable. You always put up a good argument and where did you get your enthusiasm for political debate?

If you were still working at the paper, you would have been doing an all-nighter. Watching the count and interviewing candidates and getting the latest scoop, you loved this part of your job. I miss the political energy you brought into the house. You made politics exciting and interesting and now I can't be bothered. You will be very cross to know I didn't even vote. Sorry!

It just doesn't seem important any more.

Dear Matthew,

I saw someone who looked just like you today.

I was sitting in my car waiting for the traffic lights to change and he was walking towards the train station. I prayed the lights wouldn't change quickly because I didn't want to take my eyes off this person.

He had a mop of blond hair just like you and he dressed like you and he walked like you too. He looked like a healthy version of you before your diagnosis.

I pretended for a few minutes that it was you. Just then a car horn broke my trance and I realised the lights had changed to green. As I apologised to the angry fist waving man in the car behind me, I slowly drove off trying to get a last glimpse of this young mirror image of you, but he was gone.

It was a magical moment which reminded me of what you used to look like before the cancer, before our lives changed forever. A time when my life was perfect…and then the contrast hit me. The contrast of the present moment: the reality. I wanted to escape back into that hypnotic state and pretend you were still here and that I had just seen you.

It's strange how our minds can play tricks on us!

Dear Matthew,

Your Dad and I are getting very good at looking like we are coping, and we probably are but behind closed doors we are very different people. When no one is looking we can visit that dark place called grief. It could be a memory, a feeling, a thought, or an image in our minds' eye. We can be these grieving people in front of each other but as soon as the telephone rings or the doorbell goes, we put on our coping face and a coping cloak and show the world how well we are doing. We have been practising this for a few months now and we have become experts at doing well.

Most of the time we are doing well but what does 'doing well' actually mean?

Well it has been over six months now and life has to go on, as someone reminded me the other day. Does it mean we should go back to normality now? What is normality? You being alive was normal so how can we get back to some sort of normality without you?

It is getting easier living without you but writing that makes me sad.

I got over my brother's death and my Dad's death and all the other people who have passed over. When I think about them now I don't feel sad, so when will it be okay to think about you and not to feel sad?

Even though I believe you have returned to infinite consciousness and you are experiencing pure unconditional love and that you are fine, it still hurts.

I miss the everyday moments we took for granted. Even the moments we used to get annoyed with you because you took so long in the bathroom. Sometimes you would have three showers a day which was ridiculous. You were such a clean freak and so high maintenance. I miss the times when you would wreck the kitchen just to make a sandwich. I miss you leaving your muddy football clothes on the floor by the washing machine. I miss seeing your muddy football shoes or cricket shoes just thrown by the back door leaving a trail of mud all the way through the house. I miss all the annoying things you used to do.

I would give anything to have those moments again.

Dear Matthew,

I often think about what life was like before you were diagnosed. It seems like a lifetime away now.

Life was pretty good before. Your Dad and I were about to move into a new phase of our lives where it would just be the two of us. You and Sarah were doing well in your careers and you had just landed a top job as a news editor. My business was keeping me busy and life generally was great. I used to say, "How much better can it get?" That was my mantra!

Nobody saw what was around the corner, although we knew something was wrong, we never suspected cancer.

I remember when you were sent to hospital, I thought, at last they will find out what's wrong and you will get sorted. What a shock we got.

Our worlds collapsed that day in disbelief when you were diagnosed with cancer and our lives have not been the same since.

I wish we could turn the clock back and do things differently. I wish I had gone into the GP appointments with you earlier and stressed how bad things were for you. You hadn't been to the doctors for years but then you seemed to be there every month with various symptoms. They just saw a healthy young man whose symptoms didn't add up to anything serious. We saw the signs that things weren't right, but the GPs didn't seem concerned and we trusted them. They were the experts! What did we know?

Now we know we should have questioned and pushed more. My gut feeling was that something serious was wrong, don't you just hate hindsight?

What followed your diagnosis was two years of surgeries

and treatments, stress and anxiety with a dash of hope. Even the consultant tried to take your hope away, but I wouldn't let that happen. There was always hope.

There were good times too during your last two years. Times when you could enjoy life including your holidays, golfing, cycling, cricket and song writing. Creating your album 'Fightback' was therapy for you and what an incredible CD you recorded. An album of all your own songs that chronicled your journey through illness and highlighted your positivity and creativity.

You were amazing how you dealt with everything that was thrown at you.

How did you do it?

Dear Matthew,

I haven't written for a couple of weeks but that doesn't mean you are far from my thoughts. I still think about you most of the time, but I am starting to remember the good memories now. Times when you made me laugh and the many holidays, Christmases, Birthdays, barbeques, so many special memories. It would be easy to just think about the last two years of stress and anxiety after you were diagnosed but you had twenty-five years of health so why should I focus on the last two years.

I know I can think about the difficult painful memories if I want to and there are many, but I choose to think about the good times now. I will visit those dark memories when I do my tapping therapy EFT because I know how important it is to heal and clear them. I know I can't change what happened, but I can change how I hold each painful memory inside. I can change how I feel about each one and I can change the images in my mind. These painful memories are stacked up like a set of dominoes just waiting to be dealt with.

A friend asked me the other day, "*Why don't you just let them all go*"? I didn't know how to answer that question. I know it is possible to just let the painful memories go because I am in control of my thoughts and my feelings, but I am aware that I am holding onto some resistance to completely letting go. Even though I know you are okay and you want me to just let it all go, it is me that wants to hold onto some of it. Surely it is too soon to feel okay about you not being around anymore?

I have worked on some of the big stuff. The big tsunami memories that I couldn't even talk about without crying my eyes out. I have completely knocked the emotional intensity out because when I visit those memories now, you are there smiling, and I no longer feel the negative emotion.

I had two amazing tapping sessions working with EFT practitioners where I connected with you. The first time I was tapping and working on the emptiness inside, like I felt part of me was missing. I tapped away on how I felt and after a few rounds of tapping, I tried to tune into the empty feeling again but it was gone. Suddenly I saw your face laughing at us and you were saying *"Mum, you know all this stuff, just let it go."* I felt as if you were giving me permission to just let it go and it felt amazing. The practitioner who was working with me also picked up on this. It was a real connection with you and I cried happy tears.

You always thought Tapping Therapy was a bit weird even though you had tried it on occasions, you did reluctantly admit that it worked but you also found it quite funny. Here you were laughing at us both for tapping away and you kept repeating, *"For God sake Mum, just let it go. I'm fine now. That was then but I'm not there now. I'm here and I'm fine so just let it go."*

I had another amazing experience working on another memory. I was tapping on the memory where you had to wait three hours for your pre-op tests. You were so poorly, and you deteriorated over the course of the three hour wait. None of the medical people appeared to be concerned and there seemed to be no sense of urgency. We were sitting on hard hospital chairs and you were so uncomfortable. It was such a stressful time and we were all so scared.

I was guided by the EFT practitioner to work through this memory and it was a big one for me. I remembered it in fine detail and I couldn't have gone there on my own. After a few rounds of tapping and chatting I visited the memory again and guess what, you were there. You were smiling and looking healthy and happy. You were laughing again and saying, *"Mum, come on, you know this stuff, why are you putting yourself through this again, just let it go, I'm not ill any more, it's not happening now, it's a just a memory in your head, just let it go."*

It was definitely you there speaking your mind and I loved the connection.

I transformed a disturbing memory into something amazing, but I was aware of some remaining sadness when I re-visited the memory. In my mind, I could still see all the other thirty or so patients waiting in the room. They were still there in my mind, still going through that hell. The practitioner then guided me to tap on this sadness and we transformed the memory by sending all the patients in that room, in my mind, a healing white light.

Straight after this session I had the most horrendous diarrhoea which came on suddenly. Thank goodness I was at home because it came on without any warning. I believe that it was a kind of purging or healing in some way. I had healed an extremely painful memory of you in that waiting room, and this was my body's way of dealing with it. Letting go. Clearing it out physically!

When I visit that memory now, all I see is an empty waiting room and your happy smiling face reminding me that you are not ill and you are not still waiting in that room any more. You are transformed and so am I.

This tapping session was so powerfully healing that it knocked out a lot of the emotional intensity of all the other domino memories in my mind and I can talk about them now without getting totally upset. I know there is still work to do and I will visit each memory, one at a time and heal each one until eventually I am at peace with them all. Knowing that you are there supporting me makes it an incredible journey.

I still miss you being around and that will never change. My life changed for ever the day you died, and I need to be flexible and change with it, but I will always miss you being here. There's no cure for missing you.

Dear Matthew,

Oh, my goodness, I have just had the most amazing day. This Matrix Reimprinting course has been so much fun and I haven't laughed so much for ages and guess what, I don't feel guilty for having a good time.

I have met some amazing people and one particular special lady who guided me through a session of Matrix Reimprinting which led to healing a very painful memory today.

By revisiting a painful memory, she guided me through the Matrix process and I was able to connect with you again.

Part of the Matrix Reimprinting process is to go to a happy place and imprint a new memory. My Echo (my younger self) had decided our happy place would be a music festival and you would be playing one of your songs on the main stage, but you had a different idea. You took us back to that beach in Wales where I had that mystical / spiritual experience many years ago and I observed my Echo and you walking along the beach and communicating telepathically. There were no words, but we all shared the message.

We connected to that same pure unconditional love energy that I experienced here on that beach all those years ago and you explained that this is where you are now. Not necessarily on the beach but in this energy where only love counts and nothing else matters. You explained that there is no drama, no sadness, no stress, no guilt, no negative emotions just pure unconditional love energy and total peace. It was an incredible experience which I will never forget.

I shed tears of happiness knowing that you are here supporting me and showing me the way. I am grateful for

Matrix Reimprinting and other EFT modalities for being the tool to allow me to connect with you. I do not know where I would be without them.

I was on a high driving home from the course today. The sun was shining, I could feel summer in the air and life was beginning to feel good again.

Dear Matthew,

I explained to your Dad this morning about how I connected with you in the Matrix yesterday and he listened quietly. His eyes filled up with tears and he said he was really happy for me because it was helping me, but he didn't believe in it. I said that was fine and I would probably be the same if I hadn't experienced it for myself. I said it doesn't matter though what he believes in while he is here, but once he graduates to the next level he won't be able to escape it.

It was the last day of the Matrix Reimprinting course today and it was sad to say goodbye to everyone. What a great bunch of people and what a great five days we shared together. We had such a laugh at times; there were tears as well but thankfully we have all grown throughout the process.

I love connecting with you unexpectedly through these sessions and I can feel you around me most of the time now. I just have to think about you and I sense you are there.

I have so many painful memories to work on and I wish I could just completely knock them out effortlessly. I have this new relationship with you and I know you are fine so why can't I just let them go? Do I need to visit each one individually to discover what needs to be understood and to take the learning? I am not a patient person and I just want them gone. You have given your blessing and told me to just let them go so why is it so bloody hard?

Dear Matthew,

I watched a film tonight, with your Dad, called *The Shack*. It's not your sort of film and it wasn't your Dad's either. He tolerated it for thirty minutes then announced he was going into the music room to do some recording. I think the film triggered something in him which he didn't want to admit to or deal with.

The film is about a man called Mack who sadly loses a child and questions where God was during the tragedy. That is a question that has been asked since the beginning of time. I know it sometimes comes across that God is responsible for all the good and bad in the world but it is a thought-provoking film. I didn't particularly like the religious Christian undertone to the film because it didn't include other faiths, but it could be a comfort to those who are trying to work their way through grief having lost a child. While some people rely on their faith to make peace with tragedy, I put more trust in first-hand experience.

Learning to make peace with tragedy includes forgiveness and for some this may be a step too far. I totally got the message, but I could understand how people would find that hard. For me, I connected to the deep, deep sadness but also to the contrast of the bigger picture. The bigger picture being that once we exit this life and graduate to the next level we will realise that life here is just a tiny blip of who we truly are. Our full magnificence becomes evident once we pass over.

I cried so much during this film, yet I enjoyed it at the same time. It reminded me that ultimately, we are spiritual beings having a human experience and that life is a school for our soul. Our souls have no gender, no race, no colour, no particular belief system, no religion or age and it consists of pure unconditional love. I believe that once we make peace with all our negative experiences and just feel love, we are home.

You are already there and you are experiencing yourself in all your true glory.

Even though I know this stuff, being stuck here in this time and space is hard without you.

Dear Matthew,

People say the strangest things when they try to find something comforting to say like, *"at least you had time to say goodbye"*, as if that makes it easier to bear, as if it's okay.

Some people exit this world suddenly and without warning like my brother did when I was eleven years old and, yes, it was a shock, but would it have been easier if he had suffered a long illness and then died?

I didn't get a chance to tell my brother I loved him, and I didn't get a chance to say goodbye. Would I have wanted him to go through your journey so that I could pacify myself in the knowledge that I had the time to say "goodbye" and to tell him I loved him?

My brother didn't experience an illness or cancer diagnosis along with the fear and anxiety that comes with that. He didn't slowly disappear in front us over the course of just over two years. He didn't endure the pain and suffering that ultimately led to his death. Would this have been better for him, or for us?

Someone was explaining to me the other day about a friend who had lost their son tragically in a car accident and how somehow that must be much worse. Some people do compare each death and think or say, "oh their grief must be worse".

I don't get sucked into trauma wars but at the end of the day, people are trying to make me feel better and their intentions are good.

There is no easy way to experience the death of a loved one but yes, we did get time to say everything we wanted to say, didn't we? We had enough time to say it a thousand times over, but this only matters here, because where you are, none of this is important. This is earth bound stuff.

Where you are now, only love counts. You know and understand everything where you are but we are here in the mystery of life trying to survive and still looking for the answers.

We are here getting stuck in the drama of life.

Dear Matthew,

It's been eight months now since you died, and life here on planet earth for us is still ticking along.

Going out and socialising is so hard now, especially when you bump into people who do not know that you are dead and then they ask about you. I would love to say, "Oh didn't you hear, Matthew graduated last year and is now living in the kingdom of God", but that would be a conversation killer!

Some people talk to me differently now and they don't know how to be around me, but I don't how to be around them either.

It is hard to hear about other people's lives and how well they are doing when mine has been so crap. I am pleased for them, but I don't want it in my face at the moment. I don't want to stand around and have mundane conversations with other people about everyday uninteresting topics.

I know people are walking on egg shells and I can sense the unease some people feel with me. It would be easier not to put myself in this position and stay at home where it's safe, but life has to go on.

I will continue to dress up and show up each day and shine my light. I will continue to be the best person I can be. I will deal with whatever life throws at me and use any tough experiences as stepping stones to get to the next level of my personal journey.

Dear Matthew,

It was election day yesterday and I only decided the night before who to vote for. I really missed your guidance as you were my political adviser. I wonder who you would have voted for this time because your Dad and I really struggled. Well I voted for a party I have never voted for before and it's done now. Exciting times here as Labour won the local seat. What do you think about that? You would have been in your element reporting on the election and I really miss the political energy you brought home at these times.

Dear Matthew,

Leaving our house for a week's holiday in a caravan in Westward Ho! Felt strange.

The drive down was nice as we chatted about you, life in general and other stuff. It was interesting because your Dad was not in a position where he could run off and escape to the music room if we went too deep, so I was gentle with him. He did ask at one point, "*Is it going to be like this all week?*" He couldn't avoid me on the fast lane of the M5. Mwah ha ha ha!

The caravan was in a perfect location looking out onto the beach and it had everything we needed except wi-fi. It said free wi-fi on the website but in reality, it didn't work in the caravans. It bothered your Dad more than it bothered me as I was happy to experience a week of abstinence from technology.

We went out for a run along the promenade breathing in the clean air coming in off the Atlantic and it felt amazing. I sensed you running with us again.

We could see words written into the tarmac on the promenade which when we read them, didn't make much sense but we recognised it was a verse of some kind. We attempted to read them as we ran but they seemed to be random words. When the words came to an end we saw a notice board which we stopped to read. It explained that the words were the poem "If", by the poet Rudyard Kipling. This particular poem had been requested by the community because Rudyard Kipling apparently spent several of his childhood years at Westward Ho! We realised we had been reading it back to front so on the way back we read it out loud as we ran over it.

I knew this was your favourite poem because I remember your Dad writing it out and giving it to you when you were very poorly. He was always so proud of you but especially so with the way you conducted yourself throughout your illness and he thought this poem could have been written for you.

You told your Dad it was your favourite poem and he was so pleased. It meant a lot to him. It was easier for your Dad to give you this poem rather than tell you to your face without getting emotional.

Your Dad and I felt emotional as we ran and connected with every word.

As we ran back, we read each word out loud and thought of you.

(Here is the full version)

If you can keep your head when all about you
Are losing theirs and blaming it on you,
If you can trust yourself when all men doubt you,
But make allowance for their doubting too;
If you can wait and not be tired by waiting,
Or being lied about, don't deal in lies,
Or being hated, don't give way to hating,
And yet don't look too good, nor talk too wise:

If you can dream - and not make dreams your master;
If you can think - and not make thoughts your aim;
If you can meet with Triumph and Disaster
And treat those two impostors just the same;
If you can bear to hear the truth you've spoken
Twisted by knaves to make a trap for fools,
Or watch the things you gave your life to, broken,
And stoop and build 'em up with worn-out tools:

If you can make one heap of all your winnings
And risk it on one turn of pitch-and-toss,
And lose, and start again at your beginnings
And never breathe a word about your loss;
If you can force your heart and nerve and sinew
To serve your turn long after they are gone,
And so hold on when there is nothing in you
Except the Will which says to them: 'Hold on!'

If you can talk with crowds and keep your virtue,
'Or walk with Kings - nor lose the common touch,
if neither foes nor loving friends can hurt you,
If all men count with you, but none too much;
If you can fill the unforgiving minute
With sixty seconds' worth of distance run,
Yours is the Earth and everything that's in it,
And - which is more - you'll be a Man, my son!
Rudyard Kipling

We ran along the sea front with the wind wiping away our tears.

We felt you were with us too.

Dear Matthew,

We visited St Nectan's Glen today. Do you remember we went there one New Year when we were staying in Cornwall? It has been improved since we were there last, but it hasn't lost its magical atmosphere.

Health and safety has arrived and the path has been reinforced but it has been tastefully done. There were more people there than when we visited and it doesn't feel quite as secret any more but I knew it wouldn't be long before the rest of the world discovered this hidden gem.

The meditation room is still the same and I wanted to add something for you but your Dad said we didn't need to and he was right. There are still lots of photos and remembrance trinkets of loved ones who have passed away, alongside crystals and angel figurines and coloured ribbons. Your Dad wrote something in the guest book and that's all we needed to do.

We enjoyed a cream tea in the café and we sat in the sunshine watching the various birds feeding on the crumbs around us. I wish I knew more about our British birds because there were birds today I didn't even recognise. I suppose they are drawn to the enchanting energy of this amazing place.

I felt you were with us too.

> *No coming, no going, No after, no before.*
> *I hold you close, I release you to be free;*
> *I am in you, and you are in me.*

From "No Coming, No Going," by Sr. Annabel Laity, from Basket of Plums: Music in the Tradition of Thich Nhat Hanh (2013) Parallax Press, parallax.org.

Dear Matthew,

Your Dad and I went to a play whilst on holiday in a small venue called *The Bike Shed* in Exeter. The play was called, *My World Has Exploded A Little Bit* – a logical, philosophical guide to managing mortality by Bella Heesom and it was brilliant.

The play is a deeply personal story about love and loss and both actors, Bella Heesom and Eva Alexander delivered a stunning, breathtakingly superb performance. It was funny, sad and incredibly brave and we were totally submerged into the whole experience.

Bella informed the audience, in a very matter of fact kind of way *"Everyone you love is going to die"* and although we already knew that, hearing it said out loud in the context of the play sent shivers down my spine.

The audience went from one emotion to another as the play re-counted her experience of first losing her father and then her mother. It incorporated the crazy moments you encounter along the way through the illness journey and funny moments like their ode to the NHS.

Most people would probably think we were bonkers going to a play about dying especially so soon after your death, but it was amazing. We were crying one minute and laughing out loud the next and we totally connected to seventeen step bereavement guide which Bella portrayed through her tender intimate moments, unwavering honesty and comic daftness.

Eva supported Bella by intermittently interacting with her and making us laugh out loud with her words and actions and her accompaniment on the piano created the perfect background. She proved to be a very talented musician as well as an actor as she played the piano complementing the mood of the play as it moved through different steps and phases.

We were invited to meet with Bella after the play and I got to give her a hug and tell her how much we enjoyed her play. I told her about you and how you only died eight months ago. I told her that many aspects of her play resonated with us and how we had shared similar experiences.

The play was one of our highlights of the holiday.

Dear Matthew,

On the last day of our holiday we visited St Beuno's Church in Culbone and what a special treat we had.

We spent time in the church and the churchyard, and I placed a heart shaped pebble on the gravestone of Joan Cooper, a lady whose history fascinates me.

There seems to be something special about graveyards. They are great places to go if you wish to contemplate and reflect on stuff, but this church has an extra special place in my heart. It is an enchanting magical place for me and I am mesmerised and constantly drawn back.

You were very much in my thoughts here. I know it meant a lot to your Dad too as he was very quiet and reflective. We wandered around for a while soaking up the energy and appreciating the serenity.

Your Dad was taking photos when a butterfly, a red admiral I think, landed on his shoulder. I asked him for his iPhone, so I could take a picture, but just as I got into position it fluttered off and then landed on me. I looked at your Dad and then burst into tears. "You know what this means," I blurted out. Butterflies signify transformation and I knew in that moment you were with us. The butterfly stayed on me for a minute and then fluttered off into the tree.

I believe the universe, the powers that be, God, source energy, angels or whatever calls the shots, orchestrated that very moment. We were standing in the right place at the right time so the butterfly would land on you first and then me as a reminder that you are still here with us. I could feel your presence and it felt amazing. The emotion could not be held in and we both cried and sobbed and cried and sobbed. Fortunately, we had the place to ourselves and we were able to allow the emotion to flow through us without any onlookers.

After a while, we sat in silence on the bench in the graveyard just trying to process what had happened when a tiny fluffy white feather zig zagged down right in front of our eyes and landed on the grass directly three feet in front of us. "Oh, my God," I cried, "did you see that?". How much better can it get? I thought. This is the first white feather incident I have had since you died, and the timing was perfect. I picked the feather up and put it in my handbag, but your Dad was not impressed. He stopped believing in the white feather phenomenon during your illness. (*A timely white feather which appears in unusual places, is thought to be an angel calling card*) He stopped believing in a lot of things out of this world unfortunately, but perhaps after today, with the butterfly and white feather experience, he can start to believe again. You know how much this place means to me, so to experience first the butterfly and then the white feather here, in this mystical location is mind-blowing.

We sat there in silence listening to all the sounds of nature surrounding us and we felt like we were being cradled in the arms of Mother Nature. We could hear the slight rustle of the trees in the breeze and the birds singing and we could feel the warmth of the sun on our bodies. We could hear the small stream gently meandering past and there seemed to be an extraordinary stillness and sense of peace as we sat together on that bench. It felt like everything around us down to the smallest blade of grass was with us in that moment and we could sense you there too. Oneness, that's what we felt, oneness.

Before we left, I tied a blue ribbon on the tree in the graveyard, the one the butterfly retreated to. A coloured ribbon is a physical representation of a prayer or wish in which the help of nature spirits or deities is asked for. I thought about you as I tied it to the tree and in my head, I told you I loved and missed you so much. I thanked the powers that be for allowing us to experience such a special time here. I'm not good with traditional prayers but that was good enough for me.

Walking back to the car we kept seeing a red admiral butterfly. It would flutter in front of us for a few feet then rest on the path and then flutter off again. It felt like you were still with us and you were escorting us back to the car. What a magical day.

I know we just have to think about you and you are there and thank you for the white feather.

Thank you for being there.

The Culbone Teachings

1) To know yourself, starting physically through exercises, knowledge of our own body as a physical being. Leading onto mental awareness through meditation and seeing the blocks which prevent our spiritual growth.

2) To be responsible for oneself where one is from moment to moment. Consider the vibrations given off to others by the state one is in, good or bad, calm or agitated.

3) To know spiritual reality. To be aware of oneself as both physical and spiritual beings.

4) There is a purpose, a path to everyone's life. Everyone has a golden thread to hold on to, to lead them up if they will grasp it.

5) The responsibility is personal, no dogma. You learn and teach through one's own personal experience.

Dear Matthew,

During our week away, we re-visited various places that we had been to over the years on our many holidays and remembered happy memories from times when our extended families came together.

Recollections of Combe Martin, Watermouth Cove, Lynton and Lynmouth, Valley of the rocks, Saunton Sands, Bude, Croyde, Watersmeet, Exmoor and so many other beautiful places, which I now hold close to my heart.

Even though they are happy memories, we were overcome with emotion at times. Reminiscing about your shared childhood holidays with your cousins and your sister Sarah and how well you all got on together was tinged with the sad fact that our family chain is now broken.

A week away from work and the distractions of everyday life gave us plenty of opportunities to actually talk to each other. Your Dad opened up much more and yes there were tears and moments which wouldn't have happened if we had stayed at home, but it was good to have the space and time to experience this.

Coming home felt empty after a week away in the caravan. The house reminded us that there was still a void and this new reality of life without you continues.

Dear Matthew,

Your Dad had a massive meltdown this morning. I was in the shower when he came into the bathroom and he sobbed and sobbed. I think the week away had opened up something and he needed to let it out, so I just held the space for him to do this.

It is so hard to see him like this but at the same time he needed to let it go.

We are used to the little tears that come and go and we often say to each other, "Are you having a moment?" But the big tsunami waves of emotion catch us off guard.

It is a big day for us tomorrow at your memorial cricket match and I think that has stirred up some mixed emotions as well.

Dear Matthew,

We had a lovely day today with family and friends at your memorial cricket match. It was a match between your old cricket team and the Matthew Bates invitation 1X and lots of your friends were there. Some of them were in the team even though they had not played cricket before which would have amused you enormously.

The Matthew Bates cup stood proud and shiny on the table waiting to be won, but it seems surreal that this was happening. It was a special day being surrounded by people who knew and loved you, but I remembered the last time we were here; it was your funeral, just eight months ago.

Who would have thought we would be back here smiling and sharing a day watching cricket eight months on, eh!

It was strange being back in the grounds without you there. I didn't get to watch much cricket as I was too busy talking to everyone, but intermittently I visualised you there in your whites laughing and joking with everyone. Every now and again I tried to find the old reality and picture you there on the outfield or walking out to bat. I reminisced about previous times here watching you play but I had to stop myself from getting upset.

Before the game started everyone gave you a minute's applause which made me feel emotional and proud to be your Mum. I think you would have liked that a lot. Your Dad was amazing as usual at keeping everyone entertained and organised, getting players ready to get on and off the pitch, doing the raffle and saying a few words. You would have been proud of him again today.

I still find it hard to believe that this new reality is my life now. You should be out there in your whites playing cricket with your mates.

I'm sure you were there observing the goings on from where you are.

Dear Matthew,

It feels like the day after your funeral all over again. I keep thinking about fleeting conversations I had with different people at the cricket match, remembering you and being back at the Abbey.

I went for another tapping session (EFT) this morning and I worked on another painful memory. These sessions are really helping me to get to a better place by letting go of what I hold inside. I am a work in progress and there is a long way to go yet but I am proud of how far I have come.

I hope you are proud of me too.

"It may never be enough but give the world your best anyway."

Dear Matthew,

I was thinking today about buying a new car but then I realised how difficult that would be. Although I bought the car, we used to share the upkeep and petrol costs and because it was something we shared together, it will be difficult to let it go. Maybe I will keep it for a bit longer.

Why does it feel weird and wrong to let go of stuff like the car or your possessions? Why does the attachment to these things seem so important?

You are not in your possessions or the car, you are in my heart so why does it feel so hard to part with these things?

Perhaps I just need to do it and maybe then I will realise, it's not so hard.

Maybe I'll wait a bit longer!

Dear Matthew,

I had a massive meltdown tonight, sorry!

I think I spent too much time on my own in the house today and your Dad was out gigging this evening. The house seemed so quiet and empty and I just missed your company.

Sometimes I just wish I could have another moment with you, another conversation, another glance, another hug, another joke, another laugh because I miss that physical contact so much.

Yes I know you are okay and you are in that magical place of pure unconditional love. I know you have graduated, and I can find you in my thoughts and my heart, but I am still human, I am still here. I am still experiencing the dark heavy emotions that you don't get to feel where you are. Do you still remember how they feel? Does the experience of being a human stay with you? You may be okay, but I am not okay at the moment.

Human beings are thinking machines. We can't not think. I observed my thoughts tonight and I recognised they were quite negative. Not just the usual grief and loss thoughts and feelings, but dark heavy stuff and I could feel myself being drawn into a vortex of depression. It was there waiting for me and expecting me to enter. I felt myself hovering over the precipice and monitoring the despair, misery and hopelessness that waited for me there. It almost felt like it would be easier to submit myself to this energy than it would be to carry on living one day at a time as I had been doing for the last eight months.

There was something quite comforting about slipping into this vortex of depression. It wanted to protect and love me, but I knew that if I entered this space, it would suck my energy and try and keep me there. I had to make a choice. I could carry on as I was, or I could enter the vortex of depression.

Depression looked like an easier option and losing you gave me a good reason to be there. People would understand, and I would be supported and loved.

I felt conflicted about which way to go but I felt you were there pulling me back. I heard your voice in my head telling me, "It's not always going to be like this".

My precious angel, you are forever in my heart.

Dear Matthew,

We set off after work today to attend Trew Fields Festival, a holistic health, cancer awareness, comedy and music festival in Surrey. We stayed in a hotel in Guildford and guess what number our hotel room was?

Room number 111

The number one's used to follow you around and it was spooky how many times they came up for you.

Your Dad was blown away that out of 140 rooms at the hotel, we got room 111.

I looked up the meaning of repeating ones but found lots of conflicting information. Some articles explained that repeating ones meant you were on your soul path and you were going in the right direction. Other articles reported that when you keep coming across repeating ones that it is a message to be very aware of your persistent thoughts and ideas as these are manifesting quickly into your reality. Ensure that your beliefs, thoughts and mind-sets are positive and optimistic in order to draw the energies of abundance and balance into your life.

Maybe you understand the significance of the repeating one's now or maybe these experiences are just big fat coincidences.

We particularly wanted to be at this festival because we were told by the organiser that they were going to play your music.

I met so many Facebook friends at the festival and it was great to meet these virtual people in the flesh. Some of them had cancer and some of them were in remission. It was good to connect with people who have come out the other side of a scary cancer journey.

We listened to a variety of top class speakers, ate delicious vegan food and enjoyed scrumptious healthy smoothies. To top it off, they played your music. We were so proud of you but also very emotional when we heard your music.

It was an amazing day in lots of ways and I was pleased and proud to part of it and because your music was played, you were part of it too.

Dear Matthew,

It's the day after the festival and I am still on a high. This grief journey is a funny old thing. One minute I am staring into the face of depression and today I am riding on a sea of pride and light-heartedness.

One of the speakers yesterday talked about how grief is related to love, because we grieve what we have loved so perhaps it is not such a bad thing after all!

I am determined to work through this journey and continue to process my thoughts and feelings and speed the process up. I know you would want me to be okay and most of the time I think I am, but every now and again something comes and knocks me for six and I am back at the beginning again.

I need to make up my own mantra.

Each day in every way...

Oh fuck it! Sod the mantra!

Dear Matthew,

It is crazy how I can be okay one minute and the next minute I can be swallowed up with heartache, sorrow and pain. It comes without warning sometimes. Just when I think I am doing really well and thinking about you in positive ways, I suddenly connect to the disbelief that you will never, ever come home again and it hits me. Even after nine months this still happens.

The Grass Is Green Again.

The grass in our back garden was worn from a thousand practice golf swings.
His Mum would pretend to tell him off saying that it was killing the grass,
But he would smile and carry on regardless.
"Practice makes perfect." he laughed.
He would swing his golf club at an imaginary golf ball,
And a little more grass would die as his golf swing was perfected.

Now he has gone, the grass has grown back.
Green again and reborn,
And we dream of him being here,
Hearing him laugh,
We dream of listening to the swishing sound of his golf club sailing through the air.
The grass is green again but silent.

Bill Bates

Dear Matthew,

It is the early hours of Sunday morning and I can't sleep so I am sitting here drinking tea and eating toast as I type.

My mind is imagining what it was like for other members of our family and our many friends when they heard the news about your passing. I hadn't really thought about it before. I wasn't even there when other people were told but I am able to create all these images and dialogue in my mind as to how I think it might have panned out.

Why am I torturing myself with my imagination?

I have a vivid imagination which seamlessly goes from one scenario to another as it creates how different people were told and how they would have felt and reacted. I imagined myself in their shoes. Your Grandma, Nanny, your Aunts and Uncles, your cousins, your friends and colleagues.

I could sense wave after wave of pure disbelief and deep sadness as each person received the news and I could feel their pain.

I wish I could turn my mind off tonight.

Your Dad is sleeping soundly upstairs as I type.

I thought that perhaps, if I write about it, it will help me get it out of my head. I tried to get to sleep but the tears kept coming and my pillow was soaking wet. I came downstairs and sat on the couch and cried some more. I envisaged you there on the couch with me, just like old times, chatting about deep and meaningful stuff. I imagined you putting your arms around me, telling me, "It won't always be like this".

I love and miss you so much.

I sat on the patio for a while in the rocking chair staring out into the blackness of the night. The patio was lit up by the light from the kitchen, but it felt weird sitting there in my dressing gown at 3am staring out into the garden. It was quite breezy but still warm enough to sit there for quite a while.

The night has such a peaceful energy to it and I could feel it calming me down and grounding me. It has such a wonderful stillness and it is very easy feel close to Mother Nature. I felt as if I had the night all to myself while everyone else slept.

I'm going back to bed now and I'll listen to a podcast to stop my imagination running wild again.

Dear Matthew,

Your Dad and I went into town this afternoon to pick up a couple of things and we stopped for a coffee and cake. The town was so busy and I remembered why I normally avoid coming in at the weekend. We quickly got what we wanted and then stopped at a café.

While we were sitting eating our cake we watched a young couple pushing a buggy along when they stopped to pacify the crying baby inside. The father then reached inside and pulled out the tiniest baby. It must have only been a few days old. The look of love from both parents shone through and I could almost see them surrounded by an incredible energy. A deep, deep bond that only parents know, which we experienced with both you and Sarah. It triggered that feeling in me again and I remembered holding you like that as a tiny, tiny baby and that feeling of being completely fulfilled.

Tears started to well up in my eyes and I felt so emotional watching this young couple.

You would have made a great Dad and, in that moment, it didn't seem fair that you would never experience this. Your Dad looked at me and it was obvious that he felt the same pain inside. We have become telepathic and we can feel each other's heartache in an instant. We didn't need to mention the grandchildren that should have been but will never be born or that your sister will never be an auntie.

We could mindread each other. We probably looked like a right soppy pair with tears streaming down our faces as we drank our coffees.

Life isn't fair sometimes.

We can't control everything in our life, but we can control how we feel about things and I am choosing to feel pissed off about stuff at the moment.

"Sometimes the worst place to be is inside your own head!" Author unknown

Dear Matthew,

We decided to have a barbeque this afternoon as an early celebration of Sarah's birthday. We needed to bring some laughter back into the house and we certainly did that. Sarah wanted to invite the family which was a great idea and a good distraction.

Yes, it was weird not having you around, but everyone enjoyed themselves and it was good for the family to be here. For some of them it was the first time they had been here since you passed away.

Your cousins were great entertainment and it was good for the house to experience laughter and fun again. It blew away any cobwebs.

Even when we are having fun you are never far from our thoughts and I suspect everyone else would have been thinking about you too.

Did you see us?

Where you here too?

Could you hear the laughter?

You are still very much loved and always will be.

Dear Matthew,

It is Sarah's birthday today and we planned to spend the day together. I was having a quick tidy up before leaving the house and as I was vacuuming the living room I sucked up a feather. I caught sight of it just at the moment it disappeared into the vacuum cleaner. Now how did a feather get into the living room? This is the second feather I have had since you passed away. I wondered if it was meant for Sarah because it was her birthday but surely a feather for her would have appeared in her house.

Maybe it was a message to remind me that you are here celebrating Sarah's birthday with us. Thank you.

A white feather blown from heaven,
Settled nearby on the ground.
Found in the most amazing places,
Letting you know they're still around.
They know a pure white feather,
Won't fill your soul with fear.
It's just a loving gesture,
To let you know they're near.
Don't miss these heavenly feathers,
Or the comfort that they bring.
They are sent to you with much love,
From your loved one's angel wing.
Author unknown

Dear Matthew,

I've noticed recently that I am starting to obsess about things that were happening around this time last year. It feels like I need to go through stuff in my mind to re-live the journey which eventually led to your death. It feels like it's the run down to that dreadful day. I suppose it is the mind still trying to process what happened.

The problem with this, is that the mind cannot differentiate between a thought or actual reality. It does not know if it is just thinking about it or if it is really happening.

While we think and focus on past events, our minds think we are actually there, in that moment but we recreate it through our imagination. The mind also has the ability to add or delete parts of the memory so what actually happened can become distorted.

I understand that while I focus on past events in my mind, my body experiences the thought through my emotions, so if it is a sad thought, I feel sad and if it is a good thought, I feel good.

I know all this stuff and I understand how important it is to keep my thoughts positive, but I continue to torture myself with painful memories of your journey.

Why do I want to put myself through that again?

It is not happening now.

You are not there going through that stuff now.

It is in the past, but my mind has the ability to bring it back into the present moment with my thoughts and then my physical body feels the pain again.

Nobody else puts those thoughts into my mind.

I do it to myself.

I am a thinking machine just like everyone else.

I should remember to tap (EFT) on myself when these thoughts come up but part of me wants to experience the pain again. Perhaps it seems like some weird connection to you.

I need to be more mindful of my thoughts and where they are taking me. When I find myself going over traumatic past events, it is important to notice how I feel and where in my body I feel it, so I can do some tapping (EFT) on it. I have the skill to speed up this grief process by working through each event and clearing how I hold it inside me. I do not need these negative memories to feel close to you.

These negative memories are holding me back and preventing me from moving forward in a more positive way. I accept these difficult memories are there and I will not push them down or push them away as that creates more unease within the body. I will work through each one until I get to a place when I can think about them without feeling emotionally charged. Wow, there is still so much work to do.

I must keep reminding myself that I do not need these negative memories to feel close to you.

I must be more aware of what's going on inside.

I feel an affirmation coming on...

Positive memories connect me to you.
Positive memories create good feelings inside.
Good feelings inside connect me to you.
Good feelings inside warm my soul.

Dear Matthew,

If a psychologist or psychotherapist had access to my mind they would probably think I needed help and label me with some mental disorder. I do not want to hand my mind over to some clever person who can intellectualise my thoughts and feelings and give me a label. I want to stay in control of my wellbeing.

Counselling is not my thing either. I don't need to talk about it to a stranger, when I can talk to you.

My doctor would probably prescribe anti-depressants and tell me to take some time off work, but I am working through it in my own way. I am not against medication and I know there's a place for it, but I choose to go cold turkey. That doesn't mean I am stronger than other people who take medication because there is no right or wrong way to cope with grief. I'm just doing it my way.

I know that medication is not the cure because there is no cure for missing you.

I am going to practise my happy memories today and my smiling. I am going to fully associate myself into them and feel good because this will make the connection to you even stronger.

Here goes… watch this space… just keep those people in white coats away from me…

Dear Matthew,

Practising my happy memories and listening to uplifting podcasts is really helping me. I am also going to spend time on my happy journal today too.

People will think I'm really weird though if I get too happy because they will expect me to be sad. Oh God! I just heard your voice in my head say, *"It doesn't matter what other people think".*

This morning, when I went to the loo and I heard your voice in my head say, *"For God's sake Mum shut the bloody door".* You were always nagging me to shut the door and I used to love how it annoyed you. I really do feel like I am connecting to you more and more.

I went for a long walk in a country park this afternoon. The first long walk out on my own since you left and I imagined you with me. It was so peaceful and beautiful and I only saw one other person. I remembered all the walks we used to go on during your recovery to build up your strength and it felt similar. Why have I left it so long?

Being out in nature is so healing and good for the soul. It was very windy and I didn't see any butterflies or hear many birds, but being amongst the trees and the greenery felt amazing.

I have felt more at peace today.

Dear Matthew,

I'm not sure if this is a long or short-term thing but I am feeling more at peace again today. I will accept this feeling and not look for reasons to be any other way. In this moment, I am at peace.

I can feel a beneficial shift occurring and it is probably because I have been focusing on good memories. I know the bad ones are there still and I will deal with them as I go along but I am changing my attitude. I am in control.

They say it takes twenty-one days to create a habit, so today is day one of my habit changing ways. The more I consciously practise an attitude of gratitude and focus on the good memories, I will create new neural pathways in my brain and a new way of thinking will develop naturally.

Sometimes reminiscing makes me sad but that is because I am attaching the grief to the good memory. When that memory was made, I wasn't sad. It was a good time and I felt good.

I've realised I need to fully associate myself into the good memory to really feel it again. I don't just see myself in the memory, I imagine I am actually in the memory and then I am transported back to that time and I can re-live it without feeling the sadness.

I create all this in my mind. I am not observing myself in the good memory, I am actually in that good memory. I can see it all happening around me and I can hear the sounds and smell the smells again. The grief of your passing had not been created when this memory was formed and I can enjoy the good feelings again. This helps me to connect to you now.

We choose our thoughts, but I know that grief has a sneaky way of catching you off guard. It can be a daydream, a song, a comment, a moment and it can creep up on you like your worst nightmare and overwhelm you. It is still early days yet so I am being gentle with myself and allowing myself to feel what I feel.

At the moment, I am feeling a lot of peace.

Surely this is too early on in the process to feel this.

Where are those people in white coats?

A good attitude generates a good mood,
which generates a good day,
which generates a good year,
which generates a great life.

Dear Matthew,

I had another dream last night that you were still alive. The cure for cancer had been found and I couldn't wait for you to hear the news. When I woke up this morning, I had the usual muddled, half asleep moment as I tried to make sense of what was reality and what had been a dream. Sometimes it takes a few minutes to fully wake up, but I am getting used to these moments now.

The mind can be quite cruel sometimes. It creates these fictitious scenarios in my dreams which generate hope and happy endings and when I wake up I have to figure it all out again.

Such a bummer!

Yes, life is cruel sometimes. It likes to rub salt in the wound. It likes to challenge us. It's like the school bully teasing and poking us. I know you are okay where you are, but this physical existence likes to play games and keep us guessing.

I believe this life is a school for our souls and we came here for the lessons: the good ones and the bad ones. We came here for the ride and to experience all that life can throw at us and if we can still shine our light, we are doing well. I'm just annoyed you got off the ride before me!

All that life threw at you and you were still able to shine your light. You won in the game of life.

I am still feeling peaceful even after that cruel dream. It was just another dream. I am choosing to remember you have returned to source energy, pure unconditional love, heaven or whatever it is called.

There is no cancer or illness where you are and no cures are needed. You understand everything and you have all the answers. We forget everything when we are born into this physical body and I need to trust that all is well.

I am finding peace in the mystery.

Letting Go of Who Am I? by Sarah Bates

I very recently read an article that came up on my Facebook timeline – a beautiful article about dealing with the death of a friend. It was about grief, friendship, and the pain of loss. I read it, and if I'm honest the first emotion that came up was a kind of bitter anger. I thought "You think *you're* feeling bad – how do you think their family is feeling?", as if somehow my grief was more valid than people who were friends with my brother. As if I "deserved" to feel more pain than someone else because I was related to him.

I'm not proud of that reaction. I honestly feel ashamed that I felt that way, because grief is hard and awful, no matter who you were to the person that passed. I sat with the emotion, recognising it for what it was, I realised it was rooted in a jealousy that I had for people who were friends with my brother – they knew him in a whole other way, they had a whole different series of memories about who he was. I remember looking through photographs at his funeral, seeing him drunk and on nights out with his school and university friends, and smiling because this was my brother in a way I had never seen – a regular mid twenty-year-old man who got drunk with his friends. It was funny to see him in that way; not because I didn't know he did that, but because I never saw that side of him.

I've recently had an experience where someone has portrayed me in a very different light to how I see myself. They've painted this picture of me as an unpleasant person, and this is who they believe I am. That's the box they have put me in. It's hard when you see yourself through someone else's eyes if that person doesn't "see" you in the way you hope you come across. But it also shows you that "who you *are" is fluid. "Who you are" isn't fixed; we are complicated, multifaceted people who look different depending on the lens someone else is viewing us through. We have so little control over how people see us, and relinquishing that control is... a little challenging, honestly. Trying to convince other people you're not a scary beast isn't worth it, when you could be focussing on building relationships with the people who *do* care about you.*

Looking back at the article and the feeling it brought up, I realised that I have been quite selfish about my grief. Grieving is very much a "you do you" thing, where you can't tell someone else how to do it, everyone just grieves very much in their own way. There's nothing even remotely wrong with grieving selfishly, if that's how I needed to do it. But also, I think, I've been almost keeping myself from admitting that it was more than just "my brother" that died.

He was something different to each of us, and we all knew him in our own way. But I neglected, I think, to include other people that knew him in their own way. Each individual facet of Matt's personality was reflected in each of these individuals, and each one of those facets has gone forever. To ignore the grief of people who considered him a friend, or those who considered him an acquaintance, or even those who may not have even liked him very much – is to ignore those parts of who he was.

So when I felt jealous of my brother's friends for having a different relationship with him than I did, it's almost like saying their version of him was "wrong", like who Matt was, was who I saw him as. That idea is like saying who Matt was, was a fixed identity, or like who I am is fixed and my reality is the only reality that matters. In letting go of that control – the control of how we see each other, it rubs up against that same fear of letting go of how people see me. I don't want to be seen as this awful person that the above person has decided I am, but I can't control that any more than I can control how my boyfriend thinks that I am wonderful and worth love.

We are not one person or one identity. To hold onto the idea that all we are is in who we think we are is to discredit the complexity of what it means to be human. We put so much thought into our self image, and who we want to be seen as, whether through Facebook or in how we present ourselves in the day to day. We want people to see us in this certain way, our "idealised" self and we make friends with the people who see us in the way we want to see ourselves.

But we have no control over that. And really? Who someone else sees me as is really... none of my business.

Matt connected with so many people through his own writing and his own story; he inspired people and changed lives. He was an incredible person – and he was my younger brother – and whoever he was to you, I hope you can forgive me for my selfish reaction to the grief of other people. And above all, I hope that you find some comfort in your grief. My blog, and my stories, and my illustrations can't match Matt's – we are pretty dramatically different people in outlook and writing style, but I don't want to close off my grief and act like my family are the only people who can feel sad. Sharing your grief, sharing the loss of the person he was to you is to celebrate all of those aspects of who he was. If you need me, I'll be here.

Love,
Sarah

Dear Matthew,

I haven't written for a couple of weeks as I have been quite poorly. Lots of GP appointments and a visit to A&E.

A&E brought back some memories. Times when you were rushed in with another infection or other health issue. I cried when I went through to a cubicle because I remember you being there and I remember everything. Such worrying, horrible times. You were much stronger than me though. I have been quite weepy for a while, but I think that is because I haven't been sleeping because of the pain.

Your Dad says I've lost my sparkle and I know he's right.

I missed most of the local music festival this year because of this but I did manage to get to the outside music gig in the square. I was okay for a few hours. It was good to get out and about and feel well for a while.

I was standing with friends and your Dad when one of the bands started playing, *'Bob Dylan's, Forever young'*. The words were so powerful and sung so well it touched me and suddenly I was back in the grief vortex. I took one look at your Dad and he was there too. Thank goodness for sunglasses. The tears ran down our cheeks as the crowd sang "forever young" and in that moment, I appreciated that you would always be forever young in our hearts and minds.

Wow! The power of music!

Dear Matthew,

It's your birthday tomorrow and I can't stop crying. I cried myself to sleep last night too. We are not sure what to do with ourselves but we have booked the day off so we can spend the day together. Me, your Dad and Sarah.

Should we bake a chocolate cake and sing you happy birthday or would that be wrong or too weird? Will we get a sign from you or sense you with us? Will we get a white feather? Will we see a robin redbreast? Will we have another butterfly land on us? I know if I become hyper vigilant in the hope of getting something special, I will miss the opportunity to celebrate your day, so I won't go looking. I will spend the day feeling close to you, knowing that you are there and I will enjoy your birthday and the many memories you left with us.

I may shed a tear as well.

Dear Matthew,

Twenty-eight years ago today, you arrived on planet earth and you completed our perfect family. Eight minutes past eight in the evening to be precise, nearly all the eights.

8 minutes past 8 on the 8th of the 8th 1989.

The number eight is the symbol for infinity when it's on its side and infinity is another word for eternity, endlessness, perpetuity and infinitude. Big words for me but I just checked them out in the thesaurus. Words that describe our experience from infinite source to having a human experience and back to infinite source.

Celebration of Life

Gather 'round and celebrate the joy that has been given.
A gift of love, of flesh and blood. A tiny bit of heaven.

See the wonder of it all, and marvel at the sight,
Share the happiness we know, celebrate the life.

Make memories of the times to come, of hours and days and years.
Mark down each step, each task, each word, the laughter and the tears.

For a celebration of life is such, that one must never be
In too big a hurry to stop and smell... to feel... to touch... to see.

Yes, gather 'round and celebrate the life that has been given,
A gift of love, of hope eternal. Our tiny bit of heaven.

Author unknown

I am so grateful we had you for a few years, but little did we know, we wouldn't be able to keep you forever, except in our hearts. You brought so much joy into our lives. You were our tiny bit of heaven, along with Sarah.

It was weird not seeing a pile of opened presents or seeing your birthday cards on the mantelpiece and the morning had such a strange energy to it.

I lit a candle in your bedroom.

We decided to visit the Abbey where you played cricket and where you have a memorial bench next to the cricket club house. We booked a history tour of the Abbey and enjoyed an afternoon tea in the orangery there.

As we were joining the small crowd for the history tour, Sarah felt someone push her forward. She turned around to see if it was her Dad but he was a few feet away from her, in fact nobody was in reaching distance. She felt it was you.

The tour was interesting but far too much information for my brain to soak in. Everyone who lived in the house over the years was called either Edward or Thomas and there were too many dates being mentioned for me to process it all. I appreciated the grandness of the rooms and the views over your beloved cricket pitch.

After the tour, we spent time sitting on your bench, looking out over the pristine cricket pitch and it felt strange. No cricket match today, plus it's raining but I could almost envisage a cricket match taking place. I could imagine the sound of the ball hitting the willow and the shouts from the cricket players, "howzat". Ghosts of past games and men in their whites still playing but in another dimension.

The reality was, it was an empty and silent cricket pitch

and we had wet bums because the bench was wet from the rain. Your Dad had wondered off on his own and he was slowly walking all around the pitch. We could see he was consumed with his thoughts and emotions, but he wanted to be on his own and your sister and I respected that.

We left a heart shaped pebble on the bench to let you know we'd been, even though, I'm sure you were there with us.

The afternoon tea was delicious except they ruined the scones by adding sultanas. Sarah and I completely wrecked the table with crumbs as we picked all the sultanas out before devouring them. You would have probably done the same.

Just before we left, we visited a one-thousand-year-old oak tree which stands in the grounds of the Abbey, which apparently William Shakespeare wrote a Sonnet about. It was a grand old tree and if it could talk, I'm sure it would have been much more interesting than the house tour we paid for.

While we were taking in all its beauty, a white butterfly landed on Sarah's head. I missed it, but your Dad saw it.

We came home and ate pizza for tea because that's what you would have wanted.

We had an interesting evening too. Your friends who started making a documentary film about you and the fund-raising Ajax to Ajax event phoned to say it was finished and we could watch it.

Seeing you in the film being interviewed and seeing us being interviewed brought it all back. The film has been made so well and with so much thought. It had us smiling and laughing at times and crying at others as it was very emotional and to see you on screen, on your birthday, was very special.

You have some incredible friends who raised a lot of money to support us while you were going through different treatments. The film chronicled the cycle ride from Ajax football ground in Warwick to Ajax in Holland and it has been seamlessly put together with clips of you when you were younger and the various interviews we all did. Your songs and music were skilfully added, which complemented the film beautifully.

The film obviously has a sad ending and we cried loads, but I was reminded of how calm and accepting you were of your situation. You weren't angry, scared or anything negative. You were totally at peace with your reality and that gives us some comfort.

Although the film was made to highlight the Ajax to Ajax fundraising event, it was so much more than that. It was about friendship and community and people coming together and positivity. It was an insight into your journey through cancer, but the film also highlighted how your experience rippled out into the wider community, which created an outpouring of love and support.

Watching the film was the perfect end to your birthday and I'm sure you were sitting there with us too.

Today's message on my perpetual angel calendar read:

Know that your loved ones are being taken care of.
Whether they are in the physical plane or among us in the spirit world.

Many happy returns of the day, Matthew, lots of love from Mum, Dad & Sarah xxxxxxxx

"Tears are love in liquid form."

Dear Matthew,

I knew yesterday was going to be a hard day, but I didn't realise how hard it would be. It felt very heavy and dark and empty and it didn't help that it rained all day.

I wonder what your birthday will feel like next year? After another twelve months of taking one day at a time, will it feel easier or will it always be hard?

Well that's your first birthday done and dusted but I still feel heavy, dark and empty. I need to tap on that!

It's raining again today and I'm not sure if it is the weather making me feel glum or if it is the remnants of getting through your birthday yesterday. We did have a nice day. We did things you would have liked to do and we felt you there with us.

This new reality is so hard to come to terms with. Your physical absence has left such a massive void in our lives and I'm still reeling from the disbelief that we will never, ever, see you again.

Dear Matthew,

It's been ten months now since you passed away.

The sun is shining today, and it has lifted my spirit again. I spent time in the garden painting the shed and the fence and I did some planting and I cut the grass.

The garden has been neglected over the last couple of years, but it is starting to look respectable again. I found a golf ball and a cricket ball amongst the shrubs and I never want to stop finding them. They were lying there untouched after being lost by you after what was probably a poor shot.

Over the years our garden has been a football pitch, a cricket pitch, a golf course and tennis court and I have lovely memories of you and Sarah growing up and playing here. Long gone are the swings and climbing frames and it is turning out to be a more grown up garden now but the imprint of my memories will be forever layered in my mind.

"I find peace in the mystery and trust that all is well."

Dear Matthew,

How do I feel in this moment?
I feel peace.
In this moment, I am at peace with your passing, but I know, at any moment, that could change.
It feels like a ceasefire!
I notice this moment and feel grateful. Thank you.
I feel the stillness in my mind and body. Thank you.
I sense our connection more at these times. Thank you.
I sense the serenity all around me. Thank you.
I know you are at peace. Thank you.
Today is going to be a good day.

"I choose to find peace with uncertainty.
I choose to find peace in the mystery.
I choose to find peace with what I do not understand.
I choose to find peace with the present moment."

Dear Matthew,

Each day now we are getting nearer and nearer to the anniversary of your death. I have been feeling okay these last few days but your Dad has been struggling. We seem to take it in turns.

This time last year was very stressful and we could see you were in a lot of pain and that was hard to watch. We sensed things were going in the wrong direction but we were trying everything to turn things around.

We don't have that same stress any more because it has been replaced by a different feeling, a new feeling which has no name but it reminds us that you are not here. The feeling is like a bottomless pit full of dark emotions swishing about and every now and again it will throw up a specific feeling like deep sadness or hopelessness or pain. Occasionally a good emotion comes along and diffuses the dark stuff just like an anti-acid on an inflamed stomach.

I am still learning to feel at peace consistently each and every day, but I do feel I am going in the right direction.

Your Dad explained it beautifully last night when he said some days are black and white and some days are in colour.

Today is in colour.

Dear Matthew,

Your Dad told me about a strange experience he had in the music room yesterday. He was recording a song and using your electric guitar for a guitar lead when he felt the guitar being tugged. He said he felt that it was you probably complaining about his playing. He felt you were there, and it comforted him.

It was odd to hear your Dad talk about this experience because he says he doesn't really believe in life after death any more. He needs to have these experiences to help him understand and to reinforce that you are still around.

I feel you are near, sometimes more than others and I don't need to have an experience to believe this. Both Sarah and your Dad have experienced you being there and that makes me very happy.

The sun is shining again today and it would be a great day for golf. I used to love watching you get yourself ready and carry your clubs, load the car and drive off knowing that you were doing something you loved. I was so proud of you and I still am.

I treasure these memories in my heart.

Today is in full colour.

Dear Matthew,

Life is a funny old thing. Less than a year after your passing and here I am beginning to feel more like my old self. Oh, I know only too well that this feeling can change in an instant, but I am learning to enjoy these moments.

You would not want to see any of us fall apart or dive head first into depression. I know you want us to be okay.

I recognise that in my peaceful moments, I feel closer to you and more connected.

Peace attracts peace.

I am remembering the laws of the universe.

"Shhhhh, silence is the language of the angels!"

Dear Matthew,

I sat in the garden this afternoon and just enjoyed the peace. I could feel the sun warming my body and I soaked it all in. My thoughts were about you mostly and I found myself picturing you laughing and smiling.

I glanced up at your bedroom window and saw that the sky and clouds were reflected in the pane of glass. Seeing the clouds reflected in the glass reminded me of a memory of you when you were a child of about three or four. We were in the car with Sarah and your Dad was driving. We were on a motorway in the fast lane overtaking loads of vehicles. We passed a white van and the back window reflected the sky and clouds in the glass and you said, "Look Mummy that van sells clouds". It was such a funny moment and looking up at your bedroom window today reminded me of that memory and it made me smile.

I had mixed feelings looking up at your window, but I focused on the happy memories like the time I caught you sitting on the flat roof just underneath your window. You used the house and the roof like a climbing frame and I seemed to be always telling you to get down.

Your sister wrote a blog about the view out of your bedroom window.

GRIEF IS A FUNNY THING

My parents moved into their current house when I was twelve years old in 1998. I got the second biggest bedroom and my brother got the tiny little box room. The previous owners had put in an extension from the dining room, and it made it so outside my bedroom window you could see the roof. It wasn't even slightly safe to stand on, but that didn't stop angst ridden teenage me from climbing out of the window and sitting on the roof, looking wistfully at the sky and probably writing poems or doodling. It drove my Mum up the wall because it wasn't safe, but I loved to sit out there and daydream, and the view from outside of that bedroom window was something I literally grew up with throughout my teenage years.

When I was twenty-one, I moved out and Matt moved into my room. For five years, I had a very different view when I looked out of my window, one of a very unchanging, boring, car park. I missed living in my parents' house. I never felt I could call the horrible studio apartment home, especially because the man I was living with was becoming increasingly more violent and controlling.

After I left him in November 2014, I briefly moved back in with my parents. It was difficult for many ways, as it always is after you've had your independence and then moving back in with parents. Because Matt had my old room, I moved into the tiny box room that had been his old room and for the year or so I was there I had the view of the main road to look out on. I missed my old room, and the view, but I had no real reason to go in there. I can't remember ever going into the room.

Today, I went in there for the first time in many years. I was expecting to be emotional because his ashes are in there and it was full of his things, but I didn't find that bit hard. The hardest bit was suddenly seeing the view from my old room. Remembering a time before I moved, when me and Matt were both young adults and even before that, when we were children. Before the abusive ex, before both of our cats died. I would look out of that window and watch Matt play football or cricket. This time I looked out over the room while his ashes sat behind me on the bed.

It's funny the things that trigger grief. It's strange what makes us remember hard times. Yesterday I hung out with my cousins in Manchester and before the event I was preparing myself for what I was sure was going to be a hard day, Matt wasn't there with us, where he should've been. The thing that I actually found hard was unexpected, it wasn't the fact Matt wasn't there that bothered me, but the little things that reminded me of the relationship that we had. Snippets of conversations between siblings. Shared glances between people who had shared a childhood home, shared parents. Things I think I took for granted before Matt died, things I didn't know I was going to miss. You miss the person, but you also miss who that person was to you.

People have been getting in touch with me recently about how they've recently lost their own siblings. In many of those cases, the death was sudden. In that way, I believe I was exceptionally thankful that we knew Matt only had a short time left with us. We had a chance to hold his hand, to tell him we loved him, to be with him in his last few days. I wish more than anything that we didn't have to say goodbye, but the fact that we had that chance is something I feel so, so grateful for. You hear people telling each other to make it count, to tell your loved ones how you feel, and maybe I sound like a broken record for also adding to that list of people. Maybe you've heard people say it a lot. But you know what? Do it anyway. For me.

Sarah Bates

Dear Matthew,

I am beginning to be aware that I have an inner conflict going on between two distinct parts of me, my spiritual mindset and my human mindset.

My spiritual mindset knows that you are well and in a place of pure unconditional love, but my human mindset is drawn into the drama of life and your physical loss.

My spiritual self understands the bigger picture and is at peace with your passing. My spiritual self knows there is no death, your existence continues, and it is okay for me to be happy.

My humanness misses the physical presence of you and wants to obsess over the sad, bad times and it likes to be drawn into the drama of the grief process. It is also part of our culture to feel this and I have followed this culture with my past experiences of death too. It is normal to be sad, distraught and feel and experience the heavy dark emotions. If I don't allow myself to feel all this, I will deny myself the full experience and what will I learn? This part of me believes I need to fit into the behaviour of a grieving person and only time will heal me.

Both my spiritual self and my humanness want the best for me, but they are unwittingly creating an inner conflict inside. Both sides need to come together and accept they both want the best for me, for my highest good.

I need to identify the good qualities, strengths, resources and positive intentions of each part. I need to find out what each part is trying to do for me. What is the highest intention for each part? What is its purpose?

I can feel the separation pulling me in different directions. One minute I am at peace because I understand the bigger picture and the next minute I am a in the sadness of heavy emotions. Complete opposites of each other and the contrast is palpable.

Perhaps for now, it is just important to recognise this and send both parts love.

Dear Matthew,

Sometimes when I am writing to you, the lamp on the desk flickers and I wonder if it is you trying to contact me or if it is a sign to reassure me that you are here. I like to think it is an indication that you are with me and that you are reading the letters as I write them.

Are you cringing at my grammar?

Sometimes I genuinely feel you are there next to me.

Sometimes I feel you are unreachable, but in those moments, I like to think that you are hanging out with someone else, comforting them, or maybe just enjoying the afterlife party!

"Life reveals our spirit, if we allow it."

Dear Matthew,

We went to the Cotswolds for a few days and, while we were away, it was your Dad's birthday. We stayed in a farmhouse in the middle of nowhere and it was just what we needed. It was a great space to think and connect with the stillness and to just be.

It was an emotional day for your Dad but being away from home probably made it that bit easier.

While we were there, I contemplated on my inner conflict. If only I could understand the positive intention within each part, I could do some internal work and integrate both parts and end this unease.

Whilst I reflected on my thoughts, I recognised that both parts hold a connection to you.

While I am in the feeling body and experiencing the loss, sadness and everything else that comes with grief, I am connected to you in some way. My human mindset wants to hang onto every morsel because it feels it will lose you completely without these dark emotions. It wants to keep that connection.

My spiritual mindset knows I am connected to you because I understand the bigger picture. It has a direct connection to you.

So, each part holds a connection to you and here is the magic.

The purpose for each part, is for me to feel that connection.

The highest intention of each part wants me to experience that connection.

Both parts want the same thing but they have been

pulling me in different directions and unwittingly sabotaging my success at really feeling the connection.

It is now time to integrate both parts.

I thank both parts for being there.

I thank both parts for wanting the best for me.

It is now time for both parts to work together to bring a new sense of peace and calm which will take me to the next level in my healing process.

I am ready.

I do not want to resist my heavy emotions or battle with any negative thoughts. What we resist, persists, so instead I will accept and love these different parts of me because they are my invitation to true healing.

Any negative thoughts, feelings and emotions are not here to be released. They are here for me to experience my fullness and I need to make room for them and welcome them in. The release comes in knowing that every thought, every feeling and emotion has a home and wants to be loved. I will accept them, invite them in and I will offer them love and peace.

Even when the tsunami of disbelief washes over me, reminding me that I will never experience your physical life again, which it still does from time to time, I will allow it to happen. Disbelief can come and go as it pleases. Just like sadness and all the other heavy emotions, I will let them be.

Just knowing this means I do not need to do any work.

Just allow and be present with whatever it is I am feeling.

I allow my thoughts, feelings and emotions to come and go as they please. They are all welcome here. Good, bad or indifferent, there is a home for them here.

These last ten months have been exhausting but I am at peace now with the fact that I may never get over your passing. I have also made peace with the inner conflict that was going on and I appreciate that grief is love.

I will choose to be in the present moment as much as possible, even when the present moment is hard, and I will not attempt to change it. I will send any heavy emotions love and allow them to transcend when they are ready. I will welcome them in and pay close attention to the effect they have on my physical body and I will care for them, as if I was caring for you. I will send them love. I will allow them to come and go and move through me in a safe and nurturing way. I will listen to any messages they bring and I will take the learning. They will be free to transcend in their own time and there will be no pressure from me.

There is no rule book or timescale telling me when the grief will end because there is no end. Time is infinite and I will embrace the journey.

Each emotion, good and bad, is like you knocking on the door and asking, "Can I come in please?" How could I resist and turn my back on this? Each emotion is an energy which craves love in order to move on.

I will be patient and kind and shine my light on every occasion no matter how hard it feels, because I have the capacity to assist in the healing of these dark emotions.

I am grateful for the peace this brings me.

"If light is in your heart, you will find your way home."
Rumi

Dear Matthew,

This morning, while I was dusting the shelves in the kitchen, I picked up my hedgehog ornament and something rattled inside. I took the top off to see what was inside and I pulled out your old hospital bracelet. BATES, Matthew 08-Aug - 1989 and your NHS number was printed in bold black print across the white plastic strip. I didn't know it was in there. As I held it close to my heart, I felt a surge of emotion well up in my body. I could feel the tears pooling in my eyes and the overwhelming grief in every part of me. I visualised your wrist with you wearing this and it made me feel close to you again. Your vibration was on this bracelet.

Instead of trying to resist this overwhelming feeling and before getting sucked into the drama of what happened when you were wearing it and with all the associated memories, I noticed the feeling inside me. I thought, now is the time to try a different tactic and to really notice this feeling and allow it to be there.

I then said, "*I allow this feeling inside to be here, welcome to my body, you can stay as long as you want, I love you, thank you.*"

For a few minutes, I sent this energy my love. I visualised pure unconditional love being poured from my heart into this sensation inside, as much love as I could feel and after a while I started to feel a warm glow deep inside. This warmth washed over the overwhelm of the grief feeling until my whole body felt full of love. In this moment, I felt the overwhelm transcend and the message I received was:

This sensation (grief overwhelm) *is connected to love, the same love you felt for Matthew. By sending it your love, you are allowing it to move and change and transform.*

I felt totally at peace in this moment as I received this message. I could see your smiling face in my mind's eye and I knew you were there with me.

Thank you.

After this experience of changing an overwhelming feeling of grief into pure unconditional love, I am finding myself waiting for the next grief trigger. I am feeling slightly excited that I may have found the answer to these sensations that come from nowhere. Was it just a one off?

"Come on grief, bring it on!"

I'm not saying I have found the antidote to grief, but I may have stumbled on something that certainly helps to transform the experience. I still miss you dreadfully every day but I'm missing the joy and energy and life you brought to me. I'm missing the physical experience of you being here in the present moment. Nothing will change that.

You are loved so much. Never forget that.

Next time I must remember not to put a label on the sensation, i.e. sadness, disbelief, overwhelm. I will just notice it without my mind trying to interfere with logic or labels. I will remember to tune into the feeling as an energy, because that is all it is. These sensations and feelings are just energy within our physical structure. I don't believe they are there to be disliked, resisted or blocked. They are there to transform me. Maybe these energy sensations are just different forms of love and I need to recognise this. I need to treat them like a small child and give them love and space to be.

This is one crazy journey!
Watch this space!

"Transformation is an inside job!"

Dear Matthew,

Today is another day in the life of Louise Bates and I have another twenty-four hours, another opportunity to be mindful of my thoughts from one moment to the next. Some days though it does feel like I'm walking through treacle and today is one of those days.

I have a day of clients today, but I wish I had a day of walking on a long sandy beach with the sand between my toes and the freedom to do just what I want. I don't feel like work today. My business has been slow in picking up and I am fed up with not being busy. I've lost my enthusiasm and I need that adrenalin rush of a busy day.

Gone are the days when I had one client after another but I'm not even sure I want to go back to that but a client here and a client there makes me feel more tired.

I've been feeling slightly melancholic these last few days. The heartache goes on, but it feels less so. I keep reminding myself these feelings are connected to you and I send them love and this does warm my soul. I am starting to feel more peaceful about my situation.

It's getting near the end of summer already and that always feels a bit sad, but I don't feel like it was possible to really enjoy this season with you not being around this year. The last few months weather wise have just passed me by.

It's nearly eleven months since you passed away and I am still re-playing the scenarios in my mind of what was happening this time last year. This time last year was when things really took a turn for the worse.

People have talked to me about the different stages of grief that people go through and I had no idea what they were. Perhaps if I had gone to counselling or psychotherapy,

I would have learned about them so out of curiosity I looked up the five stages of grief.

- Denial
- Anger
- Bargaining
- Depression
- Acceptance

Well none of that really resonates with me.

The five stages of grief are vocabulary that counsellors or psychotherapists like to use in order to gauge or measure where the griever is at in order to help them. To the griever they are just five words but there is so much more before, between and after each stage. There is so much more than that.

It just goes to show that everyone does this grief thing differently and you cannot put people into boxes, or maybe I am not doing this grief thing properly.

Am I Grieving correctly?

One thing I know for sure is that grief is not something we get over or release and it is not a mental illness; it is something to be incorporated into our lives. Grief is part of my life and I am growing around it.

"Don't run away from grief, o' soul - Look for the remedy inside the pain, because the rose came from the thorn and the ruby came from a stone".
Rumi

Dear Matthew,

I met someone today who lost their baby at birth. Their baby only lived for a couple of minutes and then died in their arms. I can't imagine the horror of that. It made me stop and really think about how lucky I was to have had you for twenty-seven years.

There is so much grief and loss out there. You could be standing next to someone grieving in the queue at the supermarket and you would never know.

One thing you learned was not to judge others. You looked healthy for the most part and no-one would have guessed that you had cancer or what you were going through. This made you realise that you never know what is going on for someone else and to never judge or criticise anyone.

"Don't give up, it won't always be like this."

Dear Matthew,

It is the start of a new school year and I watched the children pass by the house this morning in their shiny new uniforms. Some of them do not look big enough to be at school and it reminded me of yours and Sarah's first day at school. Sarah looked so cute in her pigtails and smart uniform, but she was ready for school and entered with cautious enthusiasm. I remember you holding my hand so tight on your first day. I could feel your trepidation, but you were very brave as you let go of my hand to enter your classroom.

That was the first time I was properly separated from you both and I was just as scared as you two. How I wanted to be a fly on the wall in your classrooms when you both started school. It didn't take long though before you found your feet and became Mr Popular. You soon settled in.

It is a good job we don't know what's around the corner.

Each day there is a trigger to feel the deep sadness of grief again. It could be the sound of an ambulance in the distance, a song on the radio or a certain smell.

Seeing the tiny children walking to school on their first day was an unexpected trigger today.

"What doesn't kill you makes you stronger."

Dear Matthew,

It's been eleven months now since you passed away. Where does the time go?

I had a massive flashback last night in the pub. We had been to hospital to visit your Nanny and that was surreal in itself. She is on the ward next to the one where you were before you went into the hospice, so walking in that direction brought back so many memories.

It was late when we left the hospital, so your Dad and I went to the pub for dinner afterwards and we sat and chatted about our memories of your time on that ward. We remembered how compassionate and caring the staff had been with you and how comfortable they made you feel. We will never forget that! The staff on that ward helped to make, what was a very difficult time, more bearable, knowing that you were in good hands. Your Dad wrote to the ward manager afterwards to say thank you.

Suddenly a memory came back to me with such overwhelming force it took my breath away and nearly knocked me off my chair. I scared your Dad half to death. When I finally managed to compose myself enough to talk, I explained to your Dad what I had remembered.

I had experienced a traumatic flashback in full colour of a memory from the time you were on this ward. I remembered a Spanish doctor wanting to talk to us away from you. He took us to the dayroom and asked us to sit down as he had a very important question to put to us. This doctor then went on to explain that you were very poorly, and we needed to consider the option of whether to resuscitate you, if needed.

It was so traumatic to even consider the possibility that you would need to be resuscitated but I remember every word that followed as the doctor talked us through all options and what would be the kindest decision. I remember both your Dad and I agreeing in the end that it would be kinder not to resuscitate you.

I had put this memory so far back in my mind, I had totally forgotten about it. Suddenly, I was remembering it like it was yesterday. I remember everything about it down to the colours of the chairs and the carpet. I remember a visitor coming into the dayroom where we were sitting and then quickly exiting as she picked up on the gravity of the conversation. I remember how professional the doctor had been and how carefully he chose his words. I remember the shirt he was wearing. I remember the hopelessness of the situation and the disbelief that it had come to this. I wanted to protect you from knowing the grimness of your predicament, but little did I know he would be having this conversation with you later that day too, and rightly so.

Your Dad tends to forget these memories or at least he thinks he does but in that moment, in the pub, I remembered everything. Your Dad has a way of deleting painful memories but it all came flooding back to me as I was halfway through my steamed chocolate pudding, in the middle of the pub. Your Dad joked that, how could I be so upset with a steamed chocolate pudding in front of me, but he was upset too. He always makes jokes because it is his way of dealing with emotional stuff. We both shared our memories of that difficult period but no-one around us in the pub seemed to notice.

Driving home in the car, I just couldn't turn the tears off. We listened to London Grammar, the new album and I imagined you were with us, sitting in the back of the car with your seatbelt on, staring out of the window listening to them too. I imagined Sarah was there beside you and we were one big happy family again.

I felt better by the time we got home and watched a bit of telly. Distraction always helps.

That was powerful flashback and I have no idea if there are any more lurking around in my head.

I suppose it is still early days yet and maybe these experiences will keep jumping out and surprising me.

I am nearly eleven months on since your passing and I recognise that I have come a long way compared to how I was in the early days. That physical pain I felt in my heart back then is now a dull ache. Sometimes it hurts more than others, but I know my heart is slowly healing. Perhaps it is safe now to experience the traumatic memories and that would explain my flashback last night. Perhaps the overwhelming grief just drip feeds me what I can deal with when I'm ready for it.

I am doing okay. This is normal. I am ready for whatever grief has in store for me. Bring it on!

"Love knows not its own depth until the hour of separation"
Khalil Gibran

Dear Matthew,

I feel like grief is a shadow following me around. I could be having a conversation with someone or watching the telly or reading a book and I have this awareness of the grief shadow. You are never far from my mind and I like that.

Grief is becoming weirdly soothing in its familiarity and I quite like this new cosy sensation. To let go of this would mean to let go of this feeling and to move towards something less familiar and less predictable, which is scary.

This is my new comfort zone and I am feeling at peace with my grief.

"The dull pain of grief is the pain of love.
The pain of love is proof I loved."

Dear Matthew,

Today I am feeling melancholic again. Even though I am coping, and I am living my life, I miss you so much still.

I am learning to laugh and smile again but all the while, there is this space within me which I think will always be there. Sometimes this space feels like a dullness and sometimes it feels like a warm glow, but I know it is a connection to you and I give it my love and I allow it to be there.

I want you to know that when I am laughing and smiling and getting on with my life, you are never far from my thoughts. I hope you are proud of me. I have done the best I could, and I have been the best person I could be.

How I wish things had turned out differently. You should still be here living your life and I'm so sorry I couldn't make that happen for you.

I know the big tsunami waves of emotion can come from nowhere and at any time and still knock me off my feet without warning, but I have come through the worst of it now. I have survived nearly eleven months and it can only get easier, surely?

I have learned so much about myself throughout this whole process and I am still learning.

I am still learning to trust in the mystery.

I am still learning how to carry on without you.

The control freak in me has learned that I cannot always control the outcome and my God I tried but most of all I have realised how strong I am.

Every time you feel inside like you can't go on,
Every time you close your eyes and picture evils won,
Every time a storm rolls by and winds they feel too strong,
Hold on, you're stronger than you know, hold on.

From the album, Fightback by Matthew Bates

Dear Matthew,

I was thinking today about how the medical people have such a huge influence on us because we have learned to trust them from an early age. The GP is the first place our parents take us to when we are feeling poorly and they make us better.

You would have died sooner without your lifesaving operation to remove your kidney and we will be forever grateful for the expertise of your surgeon. He does amazing work in the operating theatre, but he should not be allowed to talk to his patients in a consultation room. He undid all his hard work by talking to you. He was so negative. He wrote you off using phrases such as: "It's just a matter of time before the cancer comes back". "There's nothing else we can do." and "There's no hope."

When I tried to explain that we were pursuing different diets and supplements he cut me off saying, *no one should offer you false hope.* Who the hell does he think he is? He should never have said those words. There is always hope. He should never have tried to take that away from you. Hope is a mindset. Hope is hope. There is no such thing as, 'false hope'. Those two words do not go together. No hope is an oxymoron. There is always hope.

I understand that they have to explain their professional diagnosis but if they do not believe it possible to survive stage 4 cancer, then they are limited in what they can say.

We know it is possible because we have met the survivors and they are not just surviving but thriving. Why don't the consultants take heed? They may be experts in the diagnosis, but they are not experts in the prognosis.

I recently experienced the waiting game after having a

series of tests at the hospital. I was told to wait in an empty ward because the surgical team wanted to talk to me. I waited one and a half hours and during that time I convinced myself I had something seriously wrong and I went through every scenario possible. I thought, if the tests were normal, they would just send me home or say, "we'll write to your doctor." but I found myself in limbo land trying to make sense of it. Why was I sent to an empty ward? Why did I wait so long before they spoke to me? Why did the surgical team want to speak to me? I was doomed!

I thought about how you went through this scenario, time after time, after each scan or blood test. You played the waiting game many times and we watched on. We felt the anxiety watching you go through it, hoping that this time you would get some good news. Even when you were given good news, you were told it was only a matter of time before the cancer would catch up with you.

The way medical people communicate to their patients is so important and I'm not sure they realise how much damage they do with their words or the tone they use or their body language.

Our unconscious minds look for every bit of information; even more so when we are in a stressful situation. It becomes hypervigilant to every raised eyebrow, or slight facial expression which can completely contradict what is being said.

After waiting one and a half hours for the surgical team to come and talk to me, a solitary surgeon appeared. Apparently, all my tests were normal, but she wanted me to return to my GP and ask for a couple more specific tests. *"So, I'm not dying?"* I asked her and she smiled and said, *"No, you're not dying."*

It just goes to show how one sentence can create fear in

an instance. *"The surgical team want to talk to you."* I spent one and a half hours looking into my crystal ball, creating scenarios in my mind, fearing the worst and thinking, "Today they are going to tell me it's cancer." What a relief! I wish you had experienced this relief.

Hope is hope!

"If we believe that tomorrow will be better, we can cope with today".

Dear Matthew,

I haven't written for a few days because I feel like I am stagnating with not much to say.

What happened to my life?

I feel each day is passing me by and although I am functioning okay, and on the outside, I probably look fine, how can I ever really be 100% happy 24/7 – 365 days of the year, for the rest of my life?

I see other people around me living their lives with their families and I have no idea what is really going on for them. They may have the most perfect life with the most perfect family but with this new awareness I have, I know that nothing here is permanent.

I remember a time when my world was full of love and gratitude and I can't help but feel the contrast of what my life was like then and what it feels like now. I know I will never be that same person, but will I ever feel that same passion for life and be full of love and gratitude again? I have moments where I feel it coming back but it doesn't stay.

I was so naïve back then, thinking I was in control and nothing could touch me. My life was perfect, and I was in the vortex of love and light and manifesting great things. I remember telling the universe I was ready for the next level but isn't it funny that even though my life was perfect, I was still striving for more? Why did I want to go to another level when my life was perfect? Why do we constantly want more?

Little did I know that this was on the cards or even possible. People say time is a great healer and I can see how far I've come in eleven months but how much time needs to pass before I can be completely at peace with your passing?

I mean completely at peace 24/7 – 365 days of the year - for the rest of my life?

I snatch moments of peace here and there and it feels good, but it doesn't stay.

Welcome to the school of life.

Onwards and upwards eh!

"There is a voice that doesn't use words. Listen."
Rumi

Dear Matthew,

Being a Mum is one of the best experiences I have had, but to lose you, is the worst feeling in the world. Talk about one extreme to the other. The best and worst feeling.

I was good at being a Mum and it felt natural to me. From the moment both you and Sarah were born, I instinctively knew what to do. I had no apprehension about leaving the hospital and I couldn't wait to get you both home and get into my own routine.

Breast feeding was not easy, but I loved every baby stage. It was hard work at times but as you both grew up, it got easier and easier.

Yes, being a Mum was one of the proudest achievements of my life and I was blessed to have had two wonderful human beings.

I am so proud of you both.

Just before your diagnosis, you were about to buy a house and move out and I felt our work as parents was done. Sarah had already flown the nest and it was only a matter of time before you moved out too. I knew we would be around for support if called upon, but we had raised two well rounded people who were ready for the big wide open world.

I remember thinking how lovely it would be to have the house to ourselves again, just your Dad and me. I was looking forward to moving into a different era as a couple once again. We could have romantic evening meals without any interruptions and the house would stay so tidy. The washing machine would not be on all the time and to think of all the money we would save. It was starting to look exciting.

You have to be careful what you wish for!
You have to be careful what you wish for!!
You have to be careful what you wish for!!!

I felt guilty for quite a while afterwards for having these thoughts.

It was a good job you were still living at home after your diagnosis, because you needed that extra support. As a Mum, it became my priority to care and look after you and I never begrudged a minute of it.

Now it is just me and your Dad here and it's not all it's cracked up to be. Yes, the washing machine only works part time now and yes, the house stays tidy but there are no romantic meals, not yet anyway and the house is far too quiet and empty.

It felt like this a bit when you went off to university and I distinctly remember a conversation with your Dad about how it felt like a bereavement. You weren't going to just walk back into the house at any moment because you were three and half hours away at university. We soon got used to your time away at university, knowing that it would not be long before you turned up with a suitcase full of washing on your flying visits.

I loved your visits back from university. I used to get so excited and make sure the house was perfect and I stocked up with all your favourite foods. Each time you returned we could see you maturing more and more into a fine young man and we were so very proud of you.

Although the house feels empty now, it still holds the essence of you. Your man drawer is still there in the kitchen and we keep your bedroom door open. Your cricket bat is still in the dining room and the family photos adorn the walls depicting happier times. Your scarf is still hung up on the back of the pantry door and there are mementos of you everywhere. I see your smiling face in my mind's eye and I can still remember the sound of your voice, especially your laugh and I hope I always will. I carry the memories of you in my heart and I know I am only one breath away from feeling you here.

Dear Matthew,

This time last year was horrendous for us, but no one could imagine what life was like for you. You were left practically paralyzed after your spinal surgery and an infection was proving hard to treat. It was obvious that things were taking a turn for the worse.

One of my lowest points was when the physiotherapists started talking about you coming home from your surgery and needing a hospital bed and lots of specialist equipment to care for you, including a wheelchair. My heart broke for you at this point. You had already been through two years of illness and now they were talking about you being in a wheelchair. For someone so sporty this seemed like the last straw.

Watching you go through this was torture.

I remember driving home from hospital that night full of frustration and anger. How did it get so bad? The surgery was supposed to make things better not worse. I was driving far too fast and I didn't care. As I tried to make sense of the situation, the thoughts running through my mind were chaotic. I screamed at the top of my voice over and over again and I kept banging the steering wheel with my hands. I completely lost the plot that night. I could not control the surges of anger and frustration and the tsunami of tears that overwhelmed my body. God knows how I got home safe. When I think about it now, I think that was the point I realised, I couldn't save you.

I think I started grieving for you from this point. Apparently, this is called anticipatory grief. I started grieving for the loss of your physical ability and your lost vitality. Your health was deteriorating fast and there was nothing I could do about it.

I tried to be positive and upbeat with you because I wanted to protect you from my true emotions. You had enough on your plate to deal with and you didn't need to see me falling apart. I suppressed my feelings for your benefit and so did your Dad and Sarah but behind closed doors we were falling to bits.

I stopped being Mrs Positivity as the fear of losing you kicked in. I remember my mind taking me all over the place, i.e. How would you die? Would it be quick or slow? Would it be painful? Would it be at home or the hospital? How would we tell people? So many questions and horrible thoughts started to take over my thinking process.

Fear is such a powerful emotion which left me feeling totally out of control. The impending sense that I was losing you filled me with terror and dread. I was so scared for you but also scared for everyone who loved you too.

I haven't felt angry since you died because I think I went through that stage during this time. I might be wrong though. What if I haven't gone through the angry stage yet? I might be a time bomb waiting to go off. Maybe it hasn't hit me yet. How will I know when it's hit me?

Even now I still feel confused, but I must keep reminding myself to just notice how I feel from one moment to the next and not try to analyse how I am supposed to feel. What's the point of worrying about feeling this and feeling that or am I grieving correctly? I need to just focus on how I am feeling in the moment. This present moment is all there is. Yesterday has gone and tomorrow hasn't happened yet. I can't change what's happened, but I can change how I feel about it. I can change how I feel about the future too. I can have control of how I hold my feelings inside.

It's okay that I don't feel angry now.

In this moment, I feel sad for all the horrible experiences

you went through, but you are not going through them now. That was in the past. I truly believe you are okay now.

It is hard to be human sometimes. I find myself getting drawn back into the drama of what was happening this time last year by my thoughts. I replay the painful scenarios in my mind and I practise them over and over again. Some part of me attracts the trauma that comes with those thoughts.

The hospital blunders.

The conduct and poor bedside manners from some medical professionals.

The constant worry of what's next for you.

The long hospital trips and the traffic and the endless road works!

There were no days off from the pressure of stress and uncertainty.

This is all in the past and it's not happening now, except in my mind.

There were good moments too but it's hard to remember them while I am in this mindset.

There were exceptional nurses and care staff and you had your moments of true happiness during this time. I need to focus on them.

One of the nurses sent us a text at Christmas to say she was thinking about us. How nice and thoughtful was that? There are some incredible nurses in our hospitals.

I'm sure this is normal grief.

Whatever normal grief is!

Nearly eleven months on and I am still learning to live without you here.

Dear Matthew,

Your Dad and I went away for a few days to Anglesey and we stayed with your Uncles. You would have loved it. We went swimming in the sea a couple of times, played snooker, table tennis, darts and even did a bit of shooting but only at metal targets in the garden. We also went off for long walks and enjoyed meals out. I was constantly thinking about how you would have enjoyed it too.

I like to think you were there with us.

We laughed loads and we had a thoroughly splendid time but when we returned home I felt quite guilty that I had enjoyed myself so much. I know that is crazy, but I can't help it.

How can I possibly be having such a good time under the circumstances? I'm not acting like a typical Mother grieving for her son because I'm having far too much fun. I should be still publicly mourning and falling to bits surely.

I am a private person and I'm very good at keeping it together in public. Most people don't see the grieving Louise. They see what I want them to see. I've never been a public crier.

Only you know what I am really going through, as I like to protect the people around me from seeing me any other way. Sarah is good at doing that too, but I know she is struggling. It's a mother's intuition although I'm not sure how to help her. She is very deep and not good at talking about her emotions or asking for help. I'll just be here.

Dear Matthew,

We had a bit of a meltdown last night. Your Dad and I were talking about updating our will and it brought up all sorts of emotions. We found the old will which was done twelve years ago and we reminisced about what was going on for us then.

I remember saying back then that we needed to sort out a will as we weren't getting any younger.

It was a simple process as we just left everything to you and Sarah, 50/50. Wow, that seems like a lifetime ago now thinking about it. Never did we think we would lose one of our children first. We're supposed to die first.

Having you on the will does not benefit you but taking you off it is difficult.

We enter this life with nothing and we exit this life with nothing. It's just stuff.

A job for another day!

Dear Matthew,

Oh, Matt, I am so proud of you. You are mentioned in the back of Victoria Derbyshire's new book, *Dear Cancer, love Victoria.*

You had written to Victoria, praising her for publicly sharing her cancer journey after watching an extract from her video diary on the lunchtime news. Here is your message to Victoria.

To Victoria:

I've just watched an extract from your video diary on the 1pm News and wanted to get in touch to say how brilliant I thought it was.

Up until September 2014 I was also a journalist – albeit a news editor at a local newspaper – but unfortunately, I had to resign after also being diagnosed with cancer. In my case it was a rare and aggressive form of kidney cancer. I also had surgery to remove a four inch tumour in my right kidney, the kidney itself and eleven lymph nodes.

I thought for a long, long time about writing a column for the paper or doing a diary for our readers but decided against because I didn't really have the bottle to go public with the news. Unlike you!

So, I just wanted to say well done and I hope you stick with the diary in the future. I think it's a brilliant idea for someone in a prominent media position to go under the spotlight and show what it's like having cancer, but to do so in a positive light. There are so many negative adverts on TV, or stories in newspapers etc – which is understandable – but cancer IS a manageable disease and can be used in a positive fashion.

In my case, the past months have been the worst, but weirdly also the best, of my life. Good luck in your recovery and keep up the good work.

Matthew Bates x

Victoria was devastated to hear that you had passed away and she wrote a beautiful piece in her book about you. She had also read your blogs which she described as searing, beautiful, honest and warm and she encouraged others to read them too.

How good is that?

Not long after you wrote to Victoria, you started your own blog, which we will keep live for as long as possible. You did have the bottle to share your story after all. You may not have been a prominent media celebrity, but you certainly made a difference to the 50,000 plus people who read it.

You are still making an impression on this earth and you always will.

> *"Being impressive today may be forgotten tomorrow. Be impressive anyway."*

Dear Matthew,

I had never really noticed the beauty in falling leaves before.

The trees are gradually changing colour and they are letting go of this year's leaves and, although I had always admired the magnificence of this time of year, I never really noticed the delightful individuality of each leaf as it fell. I was sitting in my car in a traffic jam when I noticed them falling all around. Not even a breeze in the air as they fell so slowly, so gently and silently and I wondered… does the tree mourn for each leaf?

I didn't notice the trees changing colour last year because there was so much going on. You were very poorly and our focus was on making you as comfortable as possible. The world was still spinning but for us it felt like we were in a different dimension which consisted of nurses, doctors, anxiety, fear, desperation, frustration, hopelessness, sleepless nights, uncertainty, stress, etc. No wonder I didn't notice the leaves changing colour last year.

The trees are letting go of their leaves, teaching me to let go too.

It's a strange time of year for many reasons especially as coming into October brings the anniversary of your death much nearer but at least I have noticed the leaves changing colour this year. I am grateful for that.

There is always something to be grateful for.

"Your intuition knows the way. Follow that feeling."

Dear Matthew,

I had the strangest dream last night. I was walking down a street with you somewhere; I don't know where, but we weren't talking. We seemed to communicate telepathically, and we instantly knew how each other felt.

I connected to that lovely warm feeling that I used to get when you were a baby especially your snuggles as a toddler on the couch after your evening bath and bedtime story. I knew you could feel it too. In this dream, we went through all the different stages of your growth, from you as a tiny baby right up until your passing. We relived and experienced the deep love we shared with each other and I knew telepathically that you got this too. In the dream, time was non-existent, as we experienced our shared emotions and experiences of our lives together. I intuitively knew that we shared this experience in the dream and it seemed real. There were no words, just eye contact like we were looking into the window of each other's soul. The best way to explain it is that we became one in the dream, but at the same time I could see you and you were looking at me. It was an incredible encounter in my dream which I am finding quite difficult to explain in words.

Some feelings I had, I had never experienced before and this uneased me slightly. Could you see something in me that you didn't like or was I fearful that you would see something I wasn't proud of?

Overall, it connected me to you and I felt that unconditional love connection that we had. I didn't want the dream to end. I wanted to stay there with you and bathe in the glorious energy of pure unconditional love.

I don't know what woke me, but I found myself suddenly

wide awake. The bedroom seemed more serene than normal and it felt like you had just left the room, and the essence of you was still there.

I tried to make sense of my reality. The dream seemed like a real experience and the energy left behind in the bedroom was proof that something very special had happened.

I went to the loo, got back into bed and tried to go back to sleep but then I became overwhelmed with sadness. The contrast of being with you in my dream, bathed in pure unconditional love and now being back in my bed, back in my reality was too painful. I could not stop the tears and sobs that came out of me and I was afraid I might wake up your Dad who was sleeping soundly next to me.

I climbed quietly out of bed and went into your bedroom. I stared out of your bedroom window into the darkness of the night for a while. Through my tears, I could just see enough to make out that it was peaceful and calm outside. Not even a gentle wind. Even the weather was sleeping. I used to love this time of night, but not tonight.

I lay on your bed and I could see from your perspective what your bedroom looked like. (I have done this so many times since you've been gone.)

With tears streaming down my face, I tried to make sense of the dream. What were those mysterious feelings I felt? I had no label for them because I hadn't experienced them before. Did we truly connect on some different dimension? Were you trying to tell me something? The contrast of being with you and the beautiful connection we had in my dream and the reality of you not being here now was palpable. The connection felt broken. I started to be afraid that you were on your own. Suddenly you seemed so far away. You felt out of reach and this upset me.

I was so upset I couldn't stop crying. The lump you get

in your throat when you are upset was beginning to get noticeably painful in my throat and I felt I was starting to drown in my own tears and snot.

It was three o'clock in the morning and I tried to go back to sleep on your bed, but my mind was wide awake. I decided to distract myself on my iPad and I watched various you tube clips and listened to a couple of mindfulness meditations; then just as I was about to go back to sleep, your Dad's alarm clock went off.

I climbed back into my bed and your Dad instinctively knew that I was upset. He went downstairs, made some tea and came back to bed and we chatted. As we sipped our tea in bed, I told him about the dream and how beautiful it was but at the same time how it has left me slightly unnerved. He reassured me that you were fine and that he feels you around all the time. It was reassuring to know he feels you here, because for the last couple of weeks I have felt a bit disconnected.

My eyes are sore today from all the crying and lack of sleep and I am feeling very emotional. I am close to tears again and I can't get that dream out of my head. I keep replaying it, trying to analyse and make sense of it. Was there a message in there I needed to learn or was it just a crazy dream? It felt so real, especially the connection to pure unconditional love but it has left me with more questions.

Today is going to be a long day.

Dear Matthew,

I have been feeling okay these last few days. Yes, I know I still have moments of sadness, but I think I always will. That dream is still floating around in my mind, but the gift is the connection we had. I still feel it now.

It is becoming the norm to feel sad over the dinner table or while doing the ironing or watching the TV. Both your Dad and I are used to having these little moments and we don't make a big deal of it. This is our new normal.

When we do something out of the ordinary like a picnic, or anything different, the grief seems more intense. We are getting used to you not being here for the everyday experiences, but days out heighten the feelings of grief. I suppose in time we will get used to that too.

I have accepted that it is hard.

Dear Matthew,

I feel there is nothing to report at the moment. My life is evolving, and I am learning to adjust and fit into this new version of me. Nothing out of the ordinary. Just another day in the life of Louise Bates. Move on, nothing to see!

Dear Matthew,

I'm feeling grateful for knowing how to care for myself. I have lots of tools that I use to get me into balance. The tapping certainly helps, and I am thankful for all my tapping buddies for supporting me.

You will be surprised to know that your Dad has learned the Emotional Freedom Techniques and he now taps. You are probably laughing your socks off at us but he has come on so much since learning it.

I hope you are proud of us and I hope you feel we have managed our grief in a dignified and positive way.

You wrote with such insight and positivity and I know I can't match that. You had a natural gift for putting your experiences across in a positive and gracious way with your writing and you inspired thousands of people. I wish I had your talent.

We are doing okay and I want you to know that. We miss you dreadfully still each day, but we are functioning and living our lives as you would have wanted us to.

We talk about you every day and we think about you most of the time. That will never change.

They say time is a healer, but time doesn't do the work for us; we do! Time doesn't heal. Time is just the transport that carries us along on our journey. We may not be fully healed yet, but we are comfortable with where we are, and we accept it. So perhaps we are healed. There's no test available on whether we are healed or not healed!

The journey continues.

"It's time to trust yourself.
Forgive yourself.
Be gentle with yourself.
Listen to yourself.
No-one else can do this for you."

Dear Matthew,

Sometimes I don't know if I am just pretending that everything is okay, or whether I really am okay. I feel like an actor in a play, living my life in the best way I can. Am I just playing a character in order to survive?

Perhaps I am really connecting to my soul and becoming aware that Louise Bates is the personality that has been created from the many life experiences. My biology, my chemistry, my being, has cultivated different beliefs, thoughts and feelings but is it possible that this grief experience has opened the window into who I really am. I am more than my biology and chemistry. I am becoming more and more the observer of Louise Bates and life in general. When I get sucked into the everyday events, I put on my human space suit and live my life as Louise Bates, but I am more mindful now of the bigger picture. Life is one big play and I am one of the actors.

I knew this stuff consciously, but I can feel the shift physically now.

All the dramas and stresses of everyday life seem so futile, yet I know at any moment, I can be sucked into it. Where you are, there is just peace, bliss, serenity, joy, love, appreciation, revelation, freedom and other elements which we have no labels for and which we have forgotten about. That same energy I experienced on the beach many years ago.

Living life from this perspective is much more fun. Maybe I am dissociating myself from reality, but what is reality? Isn't this my reality?

Knowing and feeling this doesn't make grief any easier sometimes but, some of the time now, it does.

I still have moments where I miss you being around

physically so much, it hurts. I know I can vouch for your Dad and Sarah when I say this, but it is early days and it is okay to feel what we feel. I know that everyone who knew and loved you is having their experience of grief too. We don't hold the monopoly on missing you.

I am aware that I am feeling at peace with your passing more and more of the time, but I appreciate that when I'm not, that's fine too. I don't push grief away or try to resist it; instead, I embrace it and send it love.

> *"Your name is upon my tongue, your image is
> in my sight, your memory is in my heart, where
> can I send these words that I write?"*
> Rumi

Dear Matthew,

Your anniversary is nearly here, and people have been asking what we have planned for the day.

Why would we plan something and if we did what would that plan be?

Should we be sadder because it's the anniversary of your death?

Is it so engraved into our culture that we feel we should mark that day with something different?

I can't pretend it isn't another major milestone, but it is just another day. I will be what I will be and feel what I feel, and I will allow myself space to do this.

I will share the day with Sarah and your Dad and we will decide on the day how we spend the time together. If the weather is good, we will go somewhere nice and if the weather is not, we will stay at home, watch a film, play board games and eat pizza.

We will reminisce and talk about old times and you will be the focus of our attention. We will play your music in the background and we will have a good day. We will have a good day.

"Tears water our strength."

Dear Matthew,

I'm just days away from your anniversary and I'd be lying if I said I was okay. This time last year was your final week here on planet earth and what a stressful week that was. You were in the hospice and we knew your death was just around the corner. No parent should watch their child go through that. Damn it! We are supposed to go first.

I keep telling myself it will be just another day but in reality, I know it is a major milestone.

Will life feel better after this day?

Time takes us further away from that dreadful day but the fear that I might forget what you look like or sound like is palpable. I'm glad we have your CDs so we can hear your voice and we have so many photos and videos it would be impossible to forget.

But what I would give for one more conversation with you and one more hug.

I talk to you all the time and sometimes I hear your voice in my mind, but it will never be the same as having you here.

This is a hard week!

"My thoughts like clouds in the sky, let them go, let them go. Like tears in my eye, let them flow, let them flow."

Dear Matthew,

Well it's been nearly a year since you returned to infinite source energy, heaven, pure unconditional love. I still haven't decided what to call that place yet, that place we all graduate to in the end. The word heaven gives it a religious connotation, yet pure unconditional love gives it a whoo hoo meaning. I quite like, infinite source energy, at the moment. That same energy I experienced on the beach.

I wish I could go to sleep one night and wake up and realise it was all one big massive nightmare.

For fleeting moments, I pretend you are away on a gap year and that you are going to walk back through the door at any moment and say, "Hi, I'm back". You then throw down your back pack and slump on the sofa and gain control of the TV remote and ask what's for dinner.

If only!

The year has gone by so fast, yet some days have been so painfully slow.

When I think back to the day you passed away, it feels raw and not so long ago, but the journey to this present moment has been...traumatic, painful, dark, numbing, depressing, endless...I cannot describe it in one word!

One moment I feel I'm doing really well and the next moment it's right back in front of my face. It is insidious, imposing and it demands to be felt, just like a small child pulling at my clothes saying, *"I'm still here"*.

The pain of seeing you go through illness and eventually your death may fade with time, but I wonder what toll it will have on us in the long run. The strong and dark emotions can be damaging on our fragile bodies, but they are impossible to shake off quickly and I worry about how it will affect your Dad and Sarah and other members of our family and friends.

I am still searching for the answers and the reason, not being content some of the time with the mystery.

My grief is for the life I had and the person I was when you were in the physical. I am readjusting and settling into my new reality and it takes time to make peace with this new way of being.

My grief is about missing your physical presence, the sound of your voice, your smile, your humour, your laughter, your hugs, your smell, your personality, you.

My grief is a continuous journey and I appreciate it is not something I get through, it is something I incorporate into my life, a new reality which takes time to accept. I may not be fully there yet, but I am making peace with my situation and I am going in the right direction.

I am aware from moment to moment of my vibration and what I am putting out there. Sometimes I want to change it and sometimes I just notice it and send it love. And sometimes I do nothing and just feel it.

Even after nearly twelve months I still feel the disbelief that I will never, ever, ever see you again.

How did I survive this last year?

You saved me. I heard your voice when I needed to hear it.

You supported me. I could feel you at times like you were standing next to me.

You have been my therapist. Writing these letters to you has been a healing experience.

You are my angel. I could see you in my mind's eye saying, "Come on Mum, you can get through this".

Today is another day in my new reality and what I choose to think and how I choose to feel is in my control. My human experience, up to a point, is in my control but every now and then, life will throw a curved ball my way. Other people will die and other bad things will happen but that's life and I need to keep reminding myself that ultimately, I came here for this ride.

Knowing that you are here supporting me will help me get through whatever comes my way and what's the worst thing that could happen now? Losing you was one of the worst things that could possibly happen.

If I can survive this, I can survive anything.

Dear Matthew,

Today is the first anniversary of your death.

That's the first year, the first Christmas, the first New Year, the first Easter, the first Birthdays and holidays without you, done and dusted!

Am I supposed to feel worse today because it is a special date?

Why do we put emphasis on these special occasions and expect them to be more upsetting than any other day, when in reality, it is just another day? We can choose to think about your last day and replay it in our minds and upset ourselves with the memory of your last breath or we can celebrate that you have graduated to the next level. You are not in the hospice now. That's over.

I believe you are in that amazing energy I experienced on the beach and I know you are fine, and all is well. Even knowing this, I appreciate that today is a significant milestone and I can feel the unease in my body. Twelve months ago today, I held you in my arms for the last time and that was the hardest day of my life.

Where did this last year go?

It's not just another day though!

I keep thinking about what was happening this time last year and I keep replaying it in my head. Your Dad is the same and probably all the people who knew and loved you are doing the same thing today. Why am I clock watching?

We have received many cards and messages today and we are overwhelmed with how many people remembered your anniversary. One well-wisher in particular, who is a big church goer wrote, *"I feel really furious with God for letting Matthew go, and for all he suffered."*

I am not furious or even slightly angry at God and I was surprised that this person was. Religion does funny things to people, which is why I am not a big a fan of it and why I avoid it as much as possible. If I believed God was responsible for your demise, then I would probably be pissed off with him too.

Sarah shared a beautiful tribute to you on Facebook. It was a lovely short film she made of you in photographs and it was perfect. She said she could feel you there with her when she was making it. She added your song, 'Stronger Than You Know', to accompany the film, which was the icing on the cake.

I have changed so much throughout all of this; I hope you still recognise me.

I am more emotional, more aware of my spiritual connection, more empathetic, stronger, tougher and strangely comfortable with my new reality. I never imagined my life would be this way, but I am learning to make the most of it. I am less interested in the mundane everyday issues people complain about and my life is opening up in a different way.

We never know what is around the next corner and we can't always control everything, but I understand and appreciate that deep wisdom comes from these dark times.

Whatever lies ahead for me, will always be tinged with the sadness that you will not physically be part of it, but I know you will be there spiritually. You live on in my heart and you are never far from my thoughts.

I am going to be the best person I can be, and I am going forward with my life in a more positive way because that is what you would have wanted. I will not beat myself up when I find myself struggling at times and I will be open to take whatever wisdom comes my way.

There is a lesson and a gift in every situation and I will always look for them.

What Is Dying?

A ship sails and I stand watching till she fades on the horizon,
and someone at my side says, "She is gone".
Gone where? Gone from my sight, that is all;
She is just as large as when I saw her.
The diminished size and total loss of sight is in me, not in her,
and just at the moment when someone at my side says, "she is gone",
there are others who are watching her coming,
and other voices take up the glad shout, "there she comes!"
And that is dying.

Adapted from the original poem by Rev. Luther F. Beecher 1904

Dear Matthew,

This is my last letter to you.

I never really needed to write these letters to you because you never really went anywhere.

Death is nothing at all.
You have only slipped away to the next room.
I am I and you are you.
Whatever we were to each other,
That, we still are.

These letters have really been for my benefit. They have been an account of my first year without your physical presence and they have given me deep insights into my soul. These letters have helped me to move through this period of my life and I can revisit them at any time to remind myself just how far I have come.

I will call you by your name.
And speak to you in an easy way.
I will put no sorrowful tone in my voice.

I will laugh as we always laughed
at the little jokes we enjoyed together.
I will play, smile, and think of you, pray for you.
your name will be forever heard here
that it always was.
Let it be spoken without effect.
Without the trace of a shadow on it.

All that is gone is your chemistry, your biology, your skin, your bone and blood but your consciousness is infinite.

Life means all that it ever meant.
It is the same that it ever was.
There is absolute unbroken continuity.
Why should you be out of mind
because you are out of sight?

I am learning to laugh and live again, and I am discovering our connection in the peace.

You are but waiting for me.
For an interval.
Somewhere. very near.
Just around the corner
All is well.

Nothing is past; nothing is lost.
One brief moment and all will be as it was before
only better, infinitely happier and forever we will all be one
together with Christ.

Adapted from a poem by Henry Scott Holland

I will always see you in the stars and rainbows, the fluffy white feathers and visiting robins and butterflies. I will always remember that nothing is past, and nothing is lost. You have graduated to the next level, congratulations, and one day I will graduate too. You live on in the hearts and minds of everyone who loved you. Whatever we were to each other - that we still are. I am I and you are you.

I will continue to mourn my loss, but I am no longer mourning your death.

Fly high with the angels Matthew and thank you for bringing so much into my life.

THE END...oh yeah, there is no end!

PART 2

Twelve Months On:

I appreciate it has probably not been a comfortable read but I hope you can now see the contrast to how I was at the beginning.

As the year progressed, my grief weakened. Chinks of light began to shine in as I allowed myself to feel more and more comfortable with my new reality, but I know I am still a work in progress. I know it is still early days, but I am able to sense the transformation now.

"The light gets in through the cracks."

I know the experience has changed me, and change is okay. I am still finding my feet and that is okay too. I will never be the same person I was before Matthew got his diagnosis and his unfortunate death and I am accepting that. I recognise that I am not only grieving the loss of Matthew, I am also grieving the loss of the person I was before. I am learning to love and accept the person I am now. I am also grieving for the life I had before, and I am learning to accept that life is different now and different is okay.

I have grown and transformed into a different version of me and I have developed fears and anxieties along the way. I feel like I am an updated version of computer software, but as with any new system, I come with gremlins. Perhaps I'm still not even sure who this new person is yet. I have new insecurities with this update and it will take time to feel totally comfortable with who I am.

I have an inner knowing that I am going in the right direction and that life is now unfolding in a different way for me. It's my new normal, my new reality. Do I like it? If I say "yes", then it sounds like life is better now without my son and if I say "no" it sounds like I am resisting it, and what we resist persists, so I have accepted it.

We all have our own scars from the various emotional experiences and no one would come out of a deep grief experience unscathed. Rather than seeing them as scars though, I must understand that they have moulded me into the person I am today.

There are lots of different levels or types of grief, but I never want to put myself into a box. For me it is important to just notice how I feel, from one moment to the next, without putting any logic or labels on it.

I found my way of dealing with grief and writing letters to Matthew played a big part in that process. I had days when I couldn't write, or I just didn't want to write but that was fine. The letters were written in the moment and they couldn't be forced. They started off as a journal for myself to record the thoughts and feelings of my journey through grief and loss after Matthew died and it became an open account from my heart about my personal experiences and insights that I encountered along the way.

Looking back over my letters I recognise now that I did go through the various stages of grief, but I think I experienced the denial and anger before Matthew passed away. As for the bargaining, I remember talking to God and begging the angels to leave him here. I would have done anything to make that happen. Did I go through depression? Probably, although I didn't want to admit it, I knew it would only be temporary and a normal part of the process. Have I accepted Matthew's death? Most of the time I think I have, but I still have random moments of disbelief.

Losing Matthew has been the darkest period of my life, but I have learned quite a lot through it all. I know that grief is not a mental disorder and being deeply sad is not wrong. It is a normal part of human suffering.

I am not a psychotherapist or counsellor, but do I feel I am an expert in grief. I know how to produce grief and I know how to practise it and, some days, I like to remind myself that it is still there.

Life is not always a bed of roses and bad things happen. Whether it is a divorce or the loss of a job, we will feel depressed for a while. Depression is part of life. Normal human suffering is something we need to accept and work through.

Doctors like to protect people from feeling their emotional pain with medication but be aware that when we dumb down our own emotional pain, we also dumb down our sensitivity to others. My choice to not take medication was my choice alone, and it worked for me, but that doesn't mean it is the right choice for everyone.

Medication for anxiety and depression is given to people so they can function on a daily basis, but it is not the cure. There is a place for medication and there are obviously times when it is very much needed but over prescribing seems to be becoming the norm. Unfortunately, instead of being used as a stepping stone to wellness, people can sometimes be on this medication for years. I do not want anyone to think I am against medication and I would never judge anyone for taking that route, but it was my choice, not to go there. I wanted to feel every bit of pain. I wanted grief to do its worst. I wanted to be punished because I couldn't save my son. But I survived, and twelve months on, here I am and able to view just how far I've come.

Is it possible for us to see and understand the wisdom that comes from painful experiences?

Is it possible for us to imagine a time when we could

allow ourselves to accept the experience because it has the ability to take us to another level, to transform us?

Dark times and experiences can be transformative if we allow ourselves to travel gently along with the process, but is it possible that medication thwarts this from happening?

Here I am twelve months on, and most of the time I am okay.

I am back at work, which I love, but each day I still miss the physical presence of my son.

Matthew's bedroom is still full of his possessions, but a lot of his clothes have been given to his younger cousins.

How will I feel when everything has been cleared?

His books.

His university work.

His work suits, shirts, ties and shoes.

His pyjamas.

Boxers and socks.

His smellies and toiletries, etc. etc. etc.

When his room is totally empty, how will I feel?

That is another stage I need to go through but I need to remind myself that Matthew is not in these things.

I need to remember that I can connect to the essence of Matthew. I really do believe he is here in my heart. All his belongings are just a distraction.

We will keep his cricket bats, his golf clubs and his guitars. Presents that were brought for his birthdays and Christmases. One of his guitars was brought as a graduation gift. His Dad had always promised to buy him that sky blue coloured Fender Stratocaster he saw in the music shop in Brighton if he got a good degree. Matthew was so proud of that guitar.

I had a thought the other day about using Matthew's wardrobe for my clothes. My wardrobe has limited space, and everything is clumped together. I could put my holiday clothes and chunky coats and occasional clothes in Matthew's wardrobe and then I could organise my own wardrobe properly. Just thinking about this made me feel incredibly sad and guilty. Why do I feel like I would be profiting out of a bad situation?

When his room has been cleared, I might just leave it empty for a while.

Grief is an ongoing experience which, with time, does get easier.

Things will still trigger me like the relentless cancer adverts on TV or seeing someone who looks like Matthew.

Seeing his friends looking well and getting on with their lives makes me very happy because I see Matthew in them, but I am ashamed to say there is a bit of sadness there too. It makes me wonder what Matthew would be doing with his life now if he hadn't died.

I still occasionally have clients who ask how he is doing. The news of his death has not filtered down to everyone yet and that's hard.

Days will come, and days will go, and I have learned that some days will be harder than others.

I am grateful for my life and for my experience and I will do my best to live every moment and be the best person I can be.

I am going to shine my light and keep smiling and Matthew will see me and be proud of his Mum, as I am of him.

(Because I wrote about Bill and Sarah in my letters to Matthew, I thought it was important for the reader to see just how far they had come as well and their contributions here give an indication of where they are twelve months on.

Over the last year we have experienced grief very differently as a family, but we have all found writing very cathartic.)

I asked Bill to share his thoughts and feelings twelve months after Matthew's passing. These are his words.

Bill Twelve Months On:

Before Matthew was diagnosed, I distinctly remember watching a TV documentary where Richard Dawkins, the author of a book called 'The God Delusion', was on stage speaking to a group of students about religion. I remember him saying how he thought it was ridiculous that, if the bible were to be believed, God had demanded the sacrifice of Abraham's son. Dawkins said it was a disgraceful story of child abuse. I sat nodding in agreement. I thought it was a ridiculous and cruel thing to ask for. If God did this how could He ask to be loved?

The following day we discovered that Matthew was ill.

I asked myself – was Matthew's illness a punishment from God because I had the audacity to agree with Dawkins?

No, of course it wasn't, but it worried me for a long time.

Questions ran through my head.

"What did I do wrong to make Matthew ill"?

"What do I need to change in my life to make him get better"?

"If I died would God let Matthew live"?

I know that life doesn't work like that, but believe me, I would have swapped my life for his in an instant.

I tried to rationalise what had happened. I am his Dad, and my job, above all else, is to protect my family and keep them safe. I had totally failed.

I would look for a sign in answer to my prayers.

If I saw a falling white feather, I wondered if it was a message… who knows where from. God? The Universe? A higher power?

A dear friend gave me two small silver stones and I carried them around in my pocket.

Written on one was the word "Hope" and the other "Courage". They mattered so much to me and I wouldn't leave the house without them. It seems ridiculous to me now but at the time I genuinely believed carrying these stones would help. At the time they gave me hope.

I don't believe in anything now, although I still carry one of the stones around. The other I gave to someone who needed it more than I did.

Throughout Matthew's illness I found it easier for to me to live in denial, rather than face the truth.

Before his diagnosis, Louise said there was a possibility that Matthew was seriously ill. I remember saying to Louise how lucky we were. I was terrified that our happiness would be taken away. I said she was worrying unnecessarily. Matt was in his prime. He played sport three times a week, how could he possibly be ill? I was busy. I worked hard. I played the guitar, I gigged regularly. I wrote and recorded songs. Life was perfect.

Even when it became obvious that Matthew was deteriorating, and we were pushing his GP into getting something done, I still carried on, desperate to retain some kind of normality.

I was at the hospital when they told him it was cancer. Our world, the world as we knew it, stopped there and then. It was like a massive train crash. Like hitting a wall. Time stopped. It was incredulous. It still is.

Throughout his illness we saw the best and the worst of the NHS, going from one hospital appointment to another, waiting for the next scan and then the long wait for his results. Then there would be a short period of normality before another scan, and another and another. Hospital paperwork regularly went missing, faxes were lost and one consultant thought he was God.

We never gave up hope. We always believed that somehow, he would pull through, there would be a "miracle" cure, a breakthrough, a new drug and he would eventually get better and life would get back to normal.

Throughout his illness Matthew was so very, very brave. I find it very hard to comprehend his bravery. He carried on every day worrying about others. Writing his blogs, his songs, recording his music. As his body wasted away, despite his strong medication, despite his terrible pain, despite the awful side effects of the treatment, the stress, the unfairness, despite everything, I never, ever, heard him complain.

Matthew inherited his bravery from his Mum. It certainly wasn't from me.

I am so proud of Matthew, his sister Sarah and of Louise.

Louise dedicated her every waking hour supporting Matthew before his diagnosis, throughout his illness and until the last seconds of his life.

Sarah was a rock and continues to be so. She has a wise head on her shoulders. I am proud of the things she has written.

I am also proud of our friends. We were overwhelmed by their kindness.

After a year of Matthew's passing it is getting better.

I promise it gets better.

Slowly.

One day at a time.

Bill x

I also asked Sarah to share her experience. These are her words in a form of a letter to her brother.

Sarah Twelve Months On:

Dear Matty,

This is the second letter I've written to you since you passed, but the first one I've actually physically written. The other one I wrote in my head a short while after you died, and I like to think you managed to read it anyway.

It's been over a year since you've gone. It's the longest I've ever gone without seeing you in the flesh. The 2nd longest time was when I went to the US for a month, and I came back and there you were at our parents' house. In my mind, it still feels like I'm just gonna see you one day, like maybe you've had an extended holiday and we just keep missing each other. But eventually, we'll meet when I'm visiting my parents and we'll joke about how long it's been, and everything will go back to normal. Everything will go back to normal.

But that day never comes, and maybe it will a long time in the future when I eventually pass away, and maybe we'll still joke about how long it's been, and our ghosts will embrace, and you'll show me around whatever the afterlife is. Until then, I have to live with the constant black hole that has opened up in my chest ever since you passed away.

So... How are you? Is it strange looking at us all, coping and not coping in our own individual way? Is it frustrating, to watch us cry over your absence when you want to just shake us and say "Oi, I'm right here, I'm fine" but can't because to us you're not here?

We're not fine. I mean, we say we're "fine", "I'm doing okay". What does that even mean?

"Yes, I'm fine, I'm dealing with the loss of someone I've known my entire life, someone who shares all the same

experiences as me growing up, someone I had a very significant sibling bond with, but ya know, I'm doing okay, shall I make another cup of tea?"

You know what's really dumb? I had it in my head that after a year, I would be completely okay. I was soldiering on until the anniversary of your death, I was doing the very British thing of keeping calm and carrying on - I will be fine once the year anniversary is up. I held my breath for a year and a day, expecting that when I finally released it at the end that everything would wash away and I'd be used to life without you in it. And then the year passed, and so did the next day, and the next, and I took a new breath and that was just as filled with grief as the one I'd been holding for so long.

Grief doesn't really go away; there isn't a magical day where suddenly you're fine. I read somewhere that grief is "mourning a monumental life change", in other words, when we're grieving, we're mourning change. A lot of things changed when you died. There was suddenly this hole in our family that nothing could fill. People kept comparing their losses to mine, how they'd lost grandparents, or parents, and those losses were still just as painful as mine, but different. And that's the painful, isolating thing about grief – it's monumentally different for everyone. You are (were?) my younger brother, someone who knew what my parents were like (I remember the occasional shared glance, and eye roll), someone who I spent almost every day with as a kid, someone I was fiercely protective of, and knew you were the same with me. That person is gone, but the relationship is still there. It's like you've hung up the phone, but I'm still holding mine to my ear, waiting for you to say something. And sometimes I do, and sometimes it feels like I'm standing on hold indefinitely.

But sometimes... I'm genuinely okay. I can laugh again and most days I get by without crying. Sometimes it feels *like I've put the phone down and when I realise that's the case, I'm okay with that. But part of coming to terms with my grief has been realising that the phone is always there. Sometimes I'll pick it up and call you and you'll answer, and sometimes you won't, and in those moments, I like to think you're visiting someone else and keeping them company, and that's a reassuring thought.*

I guess what I'm saying is, that I miss you. I think I'll always miss you, and that's just a part of life now. You're always there at the back of my mind, or the front of it, and I keep going and walk forward, because there isn't an alternative. We are born crying, but we learn how to laugh.

Love you, bro
Sarah xx

I Believe Our Loved Ones Are In A Good Place:

I'm not a religious person but I know Matthew is in a good place. I know this because many years ago I was lucky enough to encounter a mystical / spiritual experience which took me to a place of pure unconditional love. This experience happened during a time in my life, a few years ago, when I was studying meditation. The children were very young, and I could spend the evenings studying while they were in bed. As part of the meditation course, I was introduced to the practice of, *an attitude of gratitude.* This new mindset has been one of the most life changing practices I have ever experienced.

When I started incorporating an *attitude of gratitude* into my everyday life I started to really notice the positives all around me. It helped me to put things into perspective and see any obstacles as opportunities to learn and grow.

Each day, I practised being grateful for everything, from waking up in a comfortable bed, grateful for the water in my taps, grateful for the food in my cupboards, grateful for the weather (whatever the weather), in fact, grateful for everything from the air that I breathed to the postman bringing the bills.

Showing appreciation for everything in my life from the moment I woke up in the morning until the moment I went to sleep at night, completely changed my circumstances, situations and relationships. I became much more aware of how many opportunities and possibilities there were for me and my life became magical. I focused my attention on all the good things in my life and all the positivity around me and I received more of the same back. I could feel myself changing energetically, and this influenced every aspect of my life.

Living with an *attitude of gratitude* on a daily basis and practising to be *in the present moment* as much as possible led me to experiencing the most amazing encounter of my life.

I was on a beach on holiday with my family and we had just had the most perfect day. We were just starting to pack away when we decided to go in the sea for one last dip. I remember coming out of the sea and sitting in the wake of the waves and thinking and feeling how wonderful my life was. I was so full of gratitude and love, I felt I could burst. I looked up to the sky and in my mind, I said *thank you.*

Just as I was sending out my gratitude, everything changed. I felt my energy shift and what followed I cannot properly put into words because I do not have the language to explain it. It was as if a veil opened from beyond the horizon before me and an outpouring of pure unconditional love flowed towards me and then washed over me.

The English language can be very limited sometimes, but this is the best way I can explain it:

Newborough Beach, Anglesey, Wales, UK

It was a moment where time was non-existent, as if time did not exist. It was a connection to an energy, but at the same time I didn't feel connected; I had an inner knowing that I was this energy. I AM this energy.

I recognised this energy from a time before I was born and something inside me knew I would be this energy when I'm done with this physical body, but at the same time, it was also in me in that moment.

I had an awareness that I was not really this physical body and that this world was just a tiny blip in our existence and in that moment, I knew I was this energy and I experienced my true magnificence.

I was completely at one with everything, but I don't know, or have the vocabulary to describe the experience. The words pure unconditional love does not do it justice. It was much deeper than anything I had ever experienced as a human, but I recognised it, it was who I truly was without this human entity and in that moment, I understood everything. My human understanding wants to call this energy - infinite consciousness.

It was such a truly euphoric moment that I wanted to replicate the experience, so much so, I have re-visited the same beach many times in the hope that I could encounter that moment again. It was like a drug and I needed more but eventually I began to realise this was a guiding star moment and I might never encounter it again. I now fully appreciate it was a once in a lifetime event and I am at peace and forever grateful for it as most people never get to have this opportunity. This experience showed me that there is more to life than what we see, hear, smell, touch and taste and it reinforces my belief that Matthew is in a good place.

We experience our physical world through time and our five senses and emotions but there is so much more going on that we are not aware of. Our human radar system is not in tune with the spiritual world and only occasionally, if we are very lucky, do we get a glimpse into that realm. Ultimately we are infinite beings and death only happens at a physical level because our infinite consciousness lives on.

I have been lucky enough to have had other amazing experiences throughout my life including an out of body experience when I was a teenager. I am so grateful for these experiences because they underpin my belief that we are more than our physical existence. People who are religious or who have blind faith are amazing but for me I prefer personal experiences.

I know Matthew is well, and he is in this place of pure unconditional love energy and one day we will be there too.

"The self is an artificial construction. We are the oneness of the universe."

Things That Helped Me:

Even though I believed Matthew had returned to infinite consciousness, the first three or four months were hell and I just survived each day. I didn't feel motivated to be any other way and I didn't go looking for a quick fix. I had to almost force myself to keep breathing and to put one foot in front of the other, to carry on.

Each day was a struggle, but I forced myself to get up, shower and dress.

I've never been a pyjama day person or duvet day person and it was important to me, no matter how bad I felt, I had to get up and show up every day.

These were my darkest days, but I kept reminding myself how Matthew coped with everything that was thrown at him. He used to say, "Mum if I can get through this, then so can you."

Bill went straight back to work because that was his survival mechanism. Distraction worked well for him… for a while!

It was strange how we both did grief so differently.

I didn't work during this time, so I spent most days pottering around the house and I even started decorating. The house had been neglected for a while but painting and decorating was like a therapy for me. It gave me something to focus on.

I also started writing the letters to Matthew which helped me enormously.

It was during this time that a friend of mine who also practises EFT invited me to have a tapping session with him. I said I would think about it, but in reality, I didn't really want to do it. I put it off and told him I was doing okay. I was content in my grief and nothing was going to budge me. He emailed me a couple of times, nudging me and encouraging me to see him. I eventually said I would see him and thank goodness I did.

That first session I did not know where to start. I was full of overwhelming emotions from over two years of stress, anxiety and grief. My friend, being the true professional, knew where to start and he said, "Well how do you feel?" I said, "I feel empty". And that is where we started!

That first EFT session was truly amazing. I completely cleared that empty feeling inside and I connected to Matthew. I saw his face in my mind's eye, smiling and laughing and saying, *"Come on Mum, you know all this stuff, just let it go, that happened in the past, I'm fine now, just let it go."* That was my first connection to Matthew and I was hooked. Every two weeks I returned for more tapping and I had more incredible shifts and experiences.

I am also a Matrix Reimprinting Practitioner and a few months into my grief and loss journey, I was offered the opportunity to re-take the course for next to no cost. It was a great opportunity for me to refresh my skills and it was also a nice distraction. During the course, we had lots of time to do swaps with other course members. We did plenty of work on each other throughout the five days and again I had some remarkable experiences which I have shared in my letters to Matthew.

I am also working through a home study course in FasterEFT and part of the course involves doing lots of swaps with other FasterEFT practitioners, so I was getting lots of support through this too.

I became my own therapist by using these tools on myself and I am also fortunate to know other EFT and Matrix

Reimprinting practitioners who supported me through this difficult time.

As I progress with my journey, I am safe in the knowledge that EFT and Matrix Reimprinting will help me move forward in a more positive and optimistic way.

The EFT Tapping community in general gave me enormous support. Various practitioners and training buddies really helped me to clear the traumatic memories that kept me stuck in the dark. I used EFT on the tough ones, those distressing memories I kept replaying over and over again that I couldn't get out of my head but now when I think about them, they do not stir any emotional charge inside any more.

This book is not about EFT, Tapping Therapy or Matrix Reimprinting but if you would like more information on these modalities, I have added some extra information including websites at the end of the book.

I still have memories to work on, but the emotional charge from the big traumatic ones has gone. In getting rid of the big ones, it has taken out a lot of the emotional intensity of the remaining ones still there.

I also find making a happy journal very therapeutic. I collect photos, uplifting poems and verses and anything else that makes me smile and I put them into a book. I even include notes that my hubby Bill leaves out for me including this one:

You might be nuts, but I love you very much x

The happy journal is a great resource to have out on the coffee table to remind me to be happy. Just the process of collecting such lovely things to include in the journal is very healing. When I focus on looking for happy positive phrases, poems and pictures, it creates a good feeling inside. So, the making of the journal is just as important as the journal itself. I recommend everyone does this.

At the beginning, grief can be brutal but know it will not always be like that. My main advice would be to allow yourself to feel what you feel and be gentle with yourself and as time goes by, it will ease.

When you feel overwhelmed with emotion, notice how it makes you feel and observe the sensations inside. Notice where in your body you feel it. Observe the feelings and notice if they move from one place to another, i.e. from your chest to your tummy. Do not allow your mind to control it or give it a label, i.e. sadness, anger, hurt etc. Just be the observer of the feeling or sensation.

If it feels right for you, talk to the feeling inside and say, "I allow this feeling inside to be there, welcome to my body, you can stay as long as you want, I love you, thank you."

Then send love to the sensation inside. Visualise pure unconditional love pouring from your heart and washing through you and notice what happens. Be patient. The feeling may be uncomfortable but allow it to feel safe inside as you send it love.

Just notice it, allow it to be there. Really notice it. Accept it. Welcome it in like a small child and then send it love, send it love, send it love.

This exercise proved to be very helpful to me. It transformed those emotions that were unexpectedly triggered by maybe a song on the radio, or some other sentimental moment. You know, those moments that catch you off guard! This exercise really works too. It helps to transcend the heavy emotions, leaving a warm glow inside which connects you to your loved one.

Formal mindfulness is very helpful at times. It wasn't

something I could do in the early stages of grief, but it certainly supported me on occasions and it still does.

Informal mindfulness helps you to notice the present moment and it cultivates a deeper awareness of the 'now' which connects you to your inner peace and stillness. In the early stages of grief, my 'now' was not a good place to be and I wouldn't entertain mindfulness, but it is something that helped me before and it helps me again now.

Sleepless nights are part of the grief process. It may seem like grief comes to the surface more at night and it feels worse, but the stillness during the hours of darkness amplifies our thoughts and emotions.

Listening to a relaxation audio is very soothing, especially at bed time or during those nights where you just can't sleep. Using headphones really helped me to tune in and filter out distractions.

I sometimes like to listen to podcasts when the relaxation audios don't work. Find an uplifting inspiring podcast or something that interests you, maybe gardening or cooking or fishing, whatever works for you. There are thousands of free podcasts out there which will help you to switch off and relax. It is better than lying there for hours getting upset by your thoughts and not being able to sleep. Even being able to relax, helps your body to cope with what is going on.

I practised smiling a lot too (which makes me sound completely bonkers and I probably am) but it does help. The science behind this has been proved that when we smile, messages are sent to the brain that we are happy and then the feel good chemicals are released. Endorphins flood the body changing your chemistry, which improves your mood. Don't believe me......just try it... I mean, don't try it... just do it.

I also chose a healthy belief system about death.

No one really knows what happens when we die.

Some people have beliefs about heaven and the afterlife or reincarnation and some people believe death is the end, but who really knows what happens?

There are two options, either there is an afterlife or there isn't, so why not choose a good belief anyway?

The Twins Parable:

In a mother's womb were two babies. The first baby asked the other: "Do you believe in life after delivery?"

The second baby replied, "Why, of course. There has to be something after delivery. Maybe we are here to prepare ourselves for what we will be later."

"Nonsense," said the first. "There is no life after delivery. What would that life be?"

"I don't know, but there will be more light than here. Maybe we will walk with our legs and eat from our mouths."

The doubting baby laughed. "This is absurd! Walking is impossible. And eat with our mouths? Ridiculous. The umbilical cord supplies nutrition. Life after delivery is to be excluded. The umbilical cord is too short."

The second baby held his ground. "I think there is something and maybe it's different than it is here."

The first baby replied, "No one has ever come back from there. Delivery is the end of life, and in the after-delivery it is nothing but darkness and anxiety and it takes us nowhere."

"Well, I don't know," said the twin, "but certainly we will see mother and she will take care of us."

"Mother?" The first baby guffawed. "You believe in mother? Where is she now?"

The second baby calmly and patiently tried to explain. "She is all around us. It is in her that we live. Without her there would not be this world."

"Ha. I don't see her, so it's only logical that she doesn't exist."

To which the other replied, "Sometimes when you're in silence you can hear her, you can perceive her. I believe there is a reality after delivery and we are here to prepare ourselves for that reality when it comes…"

Believe that death is just another rebirth into the next level and your loved ones are in a good place. Be open minded. Your loved ones would want you to be happy and at peace with their death just as you would want your loved ones to be.

I choose to believe we have not lost our loved ones. They have graduated to the next level and one day we will graduate too, we all will. Nobody gets out of this life without graduating eventually and some sooner than others.

You don't have to be religious or spiritual to be open minded.

Maybe you are not able to believe in an afterlife but being open to the possibility that there could be life after physical death, allows you to get some comfort from grief.

Be open minded.

I believe this life is like a school for your soul. Your soul has no gender, no colour, no age or belief system. It is not able to join a minority group and it doesn't want to fight for a particular cause. We come here to be the best we can be and to experience this thing called life. Yesterday has gone and tomorrow hasn't arrived yet and all that is real is this present moment and of course love.

I am lucky to have a large family and great friends, but people work and have busy lives. I understood they couldn't be here all the time, but I know I am loved and supported. I know I could ask them for anything and they would be here in a shot. Just knowing this helped me. Don't be afraid to ask for help and support.

Know that all the love you need is within you.

Also:

- When it feels right for you, talk to people about the person who has died and keep your memories alive.
- Talk to people about your thoughts and how you feel.
- Look after yourself by eating properly.
- When you need space to be alone - be alone.
- It may be difficult to sleep but just resting is beneficial.
- Scream and shout if you want to.
- Drink plenty of water, tears might dehydrate you.
- Give yourself time and permission to feel what you feel.
- Seek help and support if you feel you need it.
- Don't be afraid to tell people what you need.
- Write a letter to your loved one. Light a candle and hold a personal item of your loved one like a watch or a photograph and create a calm loving atmosphere; then start writing. Explain how you feel and share your thoughts. No one else needs to see this letter. It is only for you and your loved one. Or, like me, write a book!

Kind, loving words you can say when someone is grieving:

- I am sorry for your loss.
- I wish I had the right words but know I care.
- I don't know how you feel but I am here to help in anyway.

- You and your loved one will be in my thoughts and prayers.
- My favourite memory of your loved one is…
- He/she was a wonderful person.

Maybe not such kind, loving words!

- At least they had a good life.
- They're in a better place now.
- They're not suffering any more.
- I know how you feel.
- My Dad died of cancer.
- It was their time.
- There's always a reason.

Love and support can come in many ways:

- Bake a cake or prepare a hot meal.
- Take some groceries around. Food shopping can be so hard for the griever.
- Write them a letter and share your favourite memories of the deceased person.
- Offer to do their shopping or look after the children or take their dog for a walk.
- People who have been bereaved may want to talk about the person who has died. One of the most helpful things you can do is simply listen and give them time and space to grieve. Encourage the person to talk and then really listen to them.
- Contact the person at difficult times especially anniversaries and birthdays.
- Be empathetic. Empathy is an intuitive connection to the feelings and emotions of other people and it

goes far beyond sympathy. Having the emotional intelligence to empathise is often a vital first step towards any compassionate action.

(Empathy is about feeling with that other person, whereas, sympathy is about feeling for the other person.)

Losing Matthew may have been an extremely badly wrapped gift that enabled me to see that there is more to life than we see and experience on a daily basis. I have been on a very profound spiritual journey which has given me a deeper understanding of who I truly am.

I am learning to laugh again, have fun and enjoy my life because if I don't, I will be letting Matthew down. Yes, I will still have my moments of sadness and grief and yes, I will still shed a tear, particularly on special occasions and sometimes just randomly, but I know he will always be in my heart and never far from my thoughts.

I am at peace with these emotions and I send them love.

Contentment is the new black.

My Physical Symptoms Of Grief:

After Matthew was diagnosed with cancer, Bill and I became paranoid about him catching so much as a common cold or bug of some kind but remarkably during this time none of us, including Matthew, picked up any colds or bugs.

After Matthew died, I went down with every bug going and had other health issues too. One thing I did not share throughout my letters was how poorly I felt some days. I went backwards and forwards to the doctors and I even had a stint in A&E with mysterious pains.

There's nothing more harmful than the grief experience for your body and mine was well and truly battered and bruised. The strong emotions that are part and parcel of grief create a very stressful internal environment which is like battery acid on the physical body.

I understand now that it was the grief coming out in me physically and I became rundown and susceptible to everything going around.

Occasionally I still have some days where I feel overwhelming tiredness, exhaustion and restlessness and I find it hard to relax. I seem to be full of aches and pains and I get more headaches now than I used to.

Anxiety was a constant battle in the early days and sometimes I still notice an awareness of my breathing and my chest feeling restricted. I started to develop a health anxiety after seeing so much cancer and illness and I became hypervigilant to every ache or mysterious pain, convincing myself that I was ill. Fortunately, I tapped using EFT on that and nipped it in the bud before it became overpowering, but I still get days where I feel anxiety hovering.

One of the strangest experiences regarding my health

was the feeling of having a lump in my throat. Bill had experienced this for a few weeks and I suggested he went to the GP to get it checked out. The sensation disappeared after a while and he never did get it checked out. A couple of weeks after his lump disappeared, I started to get the sensation in my throat and I wondered if it was maybe a virus going around. It was strange that Bill had it first and then I had it. Like Bill I didn't go to the GP either, but I did google it! What I found out was fascinating. This feeling is commonly known as the Globus sensation and it is linked to anxiety, especially with people going through grief. It made total sense because the feeling was exactly like that lump in your throat feeling when you get upset. After discovering this little gem, the sensation magically disappeared, and I haven't experienced it again since.

You often hear about people getting seriously ill after a shock or after some kind of trauma, so, it's not surprising that grief can manifest into symptoms. This can lead to mental as well as physical pain.

In Chinese medicine, the belief is that issues with the lungs and sinuses are linked to grieving. This could be why my asthmatic symptoms have worsened then!

Stress from grief can disrupt nearly every system in your body and long-term exposure to this can lead to serious health problems. It can suppress your immune system, raise your blood pressure, increase the risk of heart attack and stroke, contribute to infertility as well as speeding up the aging process. Long-term stress has the potential to rewire your brain, leaving you more vulnerable to depression and anxiety.

Depression, grief, anxiety, etc. create a different way of thinking and it is easy to get stuck. Before we know it, our mindset has been formed and it can seem impossible to be any other way. The brain has an ever-changing potential as it develops new neural pathways depending on whatever habits we get into. Our mindset is just another habit, a way of thinking. It doesn't take long for our brains to start creating a new pattern of thinking through neuroplasticity. When our thoughts are set in stone, our minds become set.

Is it possible for you to become the observer and see what your old habit or pathway is doing in your life?

Look at your thoughts and feelings and see how your body is responding to your habit.

To create a new neural pathway, you need to shift your focus and you can do this by using your imagination.

You can choose to interrupt your dark or sad thoughts and patterns when they arise. Maybe say "no" or "cancel" when an old thought or impulse comes in, and say, "It doesn't have to be like this anymore." Then turn toward the new thought and keep on going in the right direction. Build that positive pathway.

Practising self-compassion and gratitude are powerful ways to kick start building these new pathways in your brain. Making my happy journal certainly helped me to cultivate my positive practices.

With time, it has been proved, we can literally rewire the neural pathways that control our emotions, thoughts and reactions. This means we can create new neural pathways, super highways in our brain that lead us to compassion, gratitude, and joy instead of anxiety, depression, grief, etc. We have the ability to reprogram our brain, but it requires a conscious effort to build new pathways.

The process of rewiring our brains just takes repetition.

Alternatively, you can just observe what's going on without changing anything, if that is right for you.

Moving Forward:

Sometimes I feel as if Matthew is standing next to me.

I sense him.

I visualise him in my mind's eye and I hear him talking to me.

Sometimes he visits me in my dreams and sometimes I just dream.

Sometimes I don't feel him at all.

Sometimes he feels out of reach.

Sometimes the emptiness is unbearable, and it scares me.

The thought of him being on his own is horrible, but it is just a thought… and thoughts are not real. "*I must keep reminding myself that thoughts are not real; they're just thoughts.*"

Practising mindfulness helps me to connect.

When I'm in the zone, I can almost sense him there with me, sharing the moment.

Mindfulness gives me space in between my fleeting thoughts to really notice the connection.

These last twelve months my mind has been so invested in remembering everything that happened over the period leading up to his death and then his eventual death, I didn't notice that time was passing me by. My thoughts went from one scenario to another as I remembered and re-lived everything that happened. My mind was in the process of trying to understand and make sense of what transpired and while it was busy doing this, I lost all my present moments and life just passed me by.

Our minds are good at looking back into the past, getting drawn into the events that occurred and they are experts at looking into the future too. It is harder to actually live in the moment and notice, there is no time like the present.

I am starting to be more mindful. Time slows down when we live mindfully and really notice each moment.

I am still finding it hard to sleep but occasionally I get a night where I sleep all night. Matthew is still the last thing I think about before I go to sleep but most nights now I have lovely dreams about Matthew and Sarah when they were little. Matthew is still my first thought when I wake up in the morning. Most nights I wake up at some point and he is still there.

Sometimes I dream he is still alive and then, when I wake up and the realisation that it was just a dream, knocks me for six again.

Sleep is so important towards our health and well being and when we become deprived of sleep it affects our immune system and our concentration levels but just being able to relax does help.

My appetite is returning to normal, although I do more comfort eating now than I used to.

I am still processing everything, and I am going through grief my way and that's the right way for me. I will mourn my loss forever. It is a continuous process which unfolds moment by moment and as a grieving mother, there will never be a day when I will stop loving or thinking about my son. There is no substitute for Matthew, Sarah can't have another brother and she will never be an auntie. I could also mourn for the grandchildren that will never be born, but I choose not to do this.

My grief is on-going. I am missing the physical presence of my son but my grief is also for the life I had and for the person I was before my son got ill and before he died. I am readjusting and settling into my new reality and it takes time to make peace with this new way of being. I am learning to love and accept the person I am now.

I still find it hard to feel enthusiastic about my future and I know I've lost my spark. Christmas, holidays, family time and other special occasions will always be hard because there will always be this massive hole, so it is hard to look forward to anything.

I know time will soften the harshness of grief because I can see how far I've come, and I know I am doing well. I know the moments of joy and laughter will expand and grow and I understand the passing of time will help to cultivate them. When these moments arrive, I will welcome them in and learn to stop feeling sad and guilty.

I will continue to mourn but with a greater sense of understanding and that I do have a purpose to fulfil. I have learned that bereavement is not a straight line and just when I think I'm doing okay, I might break down again. There isn't a door to magically open to find everything's okay. There is no escape, only distractions.

Fourteen months after Matthew's death we went on holiday to Lanzarote to escape a cold Christmas in England. We spent Christmas Eve on the beach with the sand between our toes, enjoying the warm sun and the freedom of being away. I couldn't fully enjoy the moment though without feeling incredibly sad about Matthew. When somebody brings so much joy into your life, it is hard to live without them.

At one point while walking in the waves, I became overwhelmed with sadness that Matthew was gone, and knowing that we would never share moments again. The tears streamed down my face. One minute I was savouring the freedom of being on an all-inclusive warm winter holiday with no cooking, no housework, no shopping or worries, to the next minute being overwhelmed with sadness. It wasn't fair. He should be living his life. He should be having fun.

I wondered if he could see me.

I wondered if he was with me.

I couldn't feel him.

Was he feeling sad too?

Sometimes it feels like he is so far away and that was one of those moments.

Bill slowly caught me up and as I glanced at him, I could see, it was obvious, he was having a moment too. He was surprised to see me upset but we seem to be so in tune with each other it's not surprising really. I asked him what triggered him, and he said it was seeing a young boy on the beach drawing lines in the sand.

As a small boy, Matthew would spend hours making patterns in the sand. They were usually cricket pitches, football pitches and athletic tracks. He would get great pleasure in creating these masterpieces and then just as much pleasure in playing in them. He would run around the athletic track, timing himself and he would get us to play cricket or football and he would throw himself fully into the role and we would all have to take it so seriously. Sarah on the other hand would be off scouring the beach for any rubbish and looking for a bin to put it in. If she wasn't saving the planet from self destruction, she would be in the sea. She was like a mermaid in all weathers. It's a shame that as she got older she became wary of the sea. Matthew on the other hand became like me, entering the water whatever the weather. He was a wild swimmer in the making.

Bill and I chatted and shared our feelings and it felt good to have each other, even more so at these times.

The next day while swimming in the sea, I felt Matthew was with us. The waves were big and scary, and I got an image of him in the waves having fun and saying, "come on Mum". It was emotionally comforting to feel his energy with us and it was Christmas day which made it even more magical. I could almost make him out in the waves, but he was so far out. He was always much braver than me and he could swim out of his depth. I wanted to shout out to him not to swim too far out but I stopped myself. As the large waves crashed over my head I kept getting fleeting images of him laughing and waving. It was just like old times.

We dressed for Christmas dinner that evening still feeling high from experiencing the energy of Matthew in the sea with us. We enjoyed our meal and champagne and we finished it off with the many deserts on offer. One of the deserts was a chocolate log and as soon as the taste of chocolate cake hit my palate, I nearly choked on my emotion. This was one of Matthew's favourite cakes and he used to love decorating the Christmas log each year. Tasting it brought all the memories flooding back. At the same time, I could see Matthew in my mind's eye telling me how lovely I looked and how proud he was of us both. It felt like a real connection with him and the tears came again. No matter how hard I tried to stop them I couldn't control the flood gates. It was an amazing experience, but they were tears of happiness.

These moments keep us going.

I accept how I feel in each moment now, good and bad.

IT IS what IT IS and I can't change what happened, but I can change how I hold it inside. I am still learning to live my life and to feel totally at peace without Matthew and I know each moment is another opportunity to be there.

I can be both positive and sad. It's a new talent!

I will choose to be in the present moment as much as possible, even when the present moment is hard, and I will not attempt to change it. I will continue to monitor my thoughts and remind myself constantly that thoughts are just thoughts and that they are not real.

I will send any heavy emotions love and allow them to transcend when they are ready. I will welcome them in and pay close attention to the effect they have on my physical body and I will care for them, as if I was caring for a small child. I will send them love. I will allow them to come and go and move through me in a safe and nurturing way. I will listen to any messages they bring, and I will take the learning. They will be free to transcend in their own time and there will be no pressure from me.

I will continue to tap using EFT on bad memories which break my peace, but I will embrace and love the generalised feeling of grief which I hold inside.

Grief is something people can't see, so on the outside, I look fine because grief is invisible.

There is no rule book or expiry date telling me when the grief will end because there is no end. Time is infinite, and I will embrace the journey.

Each emotion, good or bad, is like a small child knocking on the door and asking, "Can I come in please?" How could I resist and turn my back on this? Each emotion is an energy which craves to be loved.

I am retraining myself to focus on connection, passion, excitement, gratitude, love, flow and balance. I have been there before, and I know I can be there again one day. I have moments where I experience this, but it doesn't stay for long. I know as time goes by, the connection will get stronger.

Connection, passion, excitement, gratitude, love, flow and balance are there waiting for me, but I am sabotaging my attempts to be there fully. I am still learning and finding the answers, but I now feel it is within my reach.

I will move towards positivity and attract strong supportive friendships and keep my clan close to me. I will embrace remaining sadness and support it with love. I will continue to enjoy the moments of connection with Matthew knowing that he is always in my heart and by my side. I will be there for my friends and family and use my experience to help others. Maybe one day, just maybe one day, I will be able to feel gratitude for this whole experience. Maybe!

I have the verse – Death is nothing at all - by Henry Scott Holland pinned around my home to remind me that Matthew is not gone, he did not die and that there is absolute unbroken continuity.

I will forever mourn my loss, but no longer mourn Matthew's death.

Eighteen Months On:

As I bring this book to a close, I am still grieving but I have a new sense of inner peace. My outer world still reminds me of the aftermath of Matthews death but inside I know, all is well.

Life on planet earth goes on but my therapy work has been slow to pick up and not all of my clients have come back to me. They have either found another therapist or they feel uncomfortable with my situation. I feel the latter is true. After two years of cancelling or postponing clients due to an unexpected symptom, blood test or other medical emergency with Matthew, clients look elsewhere eventually, and I don't blame them. Also, people don't know what to say and I understand that too. It is easier to avoid me than it is to have an awkward conversation. I am grateful to the clients who have stayed with me throughout and many of them have become friends. I have quiet days and I have busy days and I have learned to appreciate whatever comes my way. I like it when it's quiet and I like it when it's busy too. I wouldn't want to be busy all the time and I wouldn't want to be quiet all the time either, so I'm happy with how it is. I am feeling more content with my life. Happiness is not far away but neither is sadness. Being in a neutral place seems to be my default setting at the moment and I'm okay with this.

The flashbacks are still coming. The latest one was a memory of walking past Matthew's bedroom door and seeing him sitting on the side of his bed with his head in his hands. I asked him if he was okay and he replied, "Look at this Mum."

As I walked into his bedroom, he was staring at his bare legs. He was wearing his white towelling dressing gown after just having had a shower and I stared at his legs with disbelief. They were so very thin. We knew he had lost weight, but I was so used to seeing him in tracky bottoms or trousers that I had no idea just how thin he had become. I didn't want him to see the shock on my face, so I pretended to look neutral. "Hey Matt" I said in a soothing voice. "It's not always going to be like this. You are going to get better. This is just part of the process. Look at how well you're doing." I sat on the bed next to him and I put my arm around him but inside I was terrified. This was evidence that he was slowly disappearing in front of my eyes. He looked at me and said, "They don't look like my legs do they, Mum?"

My automatic nature was to be positive but perhaps I should have just said, "No Matt, they don't look like your legs." Maybe I should have just been there and held him but no, the only way I could manage that moment was to be positive. I was always so annoyingly bloody positive. Most of the time I believed what I was saying but sometimes I didn't, and in that moment, we were both scared. I remember holding him so tight.

This flashback bothered me for a while, but I did some serious tapping to remove the emotional charge inside that showed up every time this thought came up. When I think about that memory now, I feel more neutral about it. It's still sad and always will be but I won't allow these thoughts to haunt me. I have so many wonderful memories and I need to focus on them.

Flashbacks come and go and I'm sure there will be more to come.

I cleared out his bedroom a few days ago. Whatever was left, after family and friends took what they wanted, I took to a charity shop. That was hard, but it was important everyone got what they wanted! All that is left is his university work and a few bits and bobs at the top of his wardrobe that no-one will want. All his belongings including books, DVDS and games, clothes, shoes, coats, etc. all gone. I'll get rid of the rest another day. His bedroom is like an empty shell now. This will take some getting used to, but it needed to be done. Sarah no longer lives here, and we have nothing of hers in her bedroom. I know there's more stuff in the attic. Stuff from when he was younger. Stuff that we could have handed on to his children. God, it's so hard!

Eighteen months on and not a single hour goes by where I don't think about Matthew still. I could be having a conversation with a friend, watching TV or reading a book and my mind is constantly looking for references to think about Matthew.

Bill and I went on a bluebell walk the other day. We had done this walk with Matthew and Sarah many times to Hampton Wood over the years. It is such a peaceful and tranquil place and we had it all to ourselves. Seeing the carpet of bluebells throughout the woods looked mystical and magical. The haze of blue looked so beautiful and serene and the sounds of the birds singing created a wonderful soundscape. Each year I appreciate the bluebells in this wood it as if it were the first time.

The wood stands here all year round, in all weathers, through the winter, spring, summer and autumn. Whatever is thrown at it, it stands strong and this thought reminded me of the mountain meditation I learned while on a mindfulness course. By becoming the mountain in the meditation, we can link with its strength and stability and adopt this energy for ourselves. The same can be said for Hampton Wood.

The wood is beautiful and grounded as it experiences change from one moment to the next. It remains still as the seasons flow into one another and as the weather changes moment by moment and from day to night, the wood remains still and peaceful. In any season, it may find itself at times pelted by freezing rain, or full of fog and mist, or baking in the summer sun, or damaged by strong winds. None of this matter to Hampton Wood as it remains neutral always. The beauty of this place is not changed one bit by whether people see it or not. Seen or not seen, in the clouds or in the sun, day or night, it just is, being itself. Through it all, it just sits in the landscape. Spring comes, trees leaf out, flowers bloom and birds sing. Streams flow and Hampton wood continues to just be. Through it all, Hampton wood continues to sit unmoved by the weather, by what happens on the surface, by the world of appearance, remaining its essential self, throughout all the seasons, the changing weather, the activity ebbing and flowing throughout the woods, all is well, always.

As we walked through the woods we talked and cried and walked and talked and cried some more. The woods still sitting unchanging by our presence.

We encounter storms of different intensities in our outer world and in our own minds and bodies. We get buffeted by high winds and cold rain. We endure periods of darkness and pain as well as moments of joy and bliss. By becoming Hampton wood, we can link with its strength and stability and adopt this way of being for ourselves. We can use its energies to support us too.

I am learning to embody the same centred, unwavering, stillness in the face of everything that grief has brought into my life.

Eighteen months on and it is getting easier. I know how important it is to keep myself grounded and remember that thoughts are just thoughts, they are not facts and they are not real.

I recently qualified as a Mindfulness teacher and this course has helped me to cultivate this new awareness. It has been a great support through these last few months and it will continue to strengthen my emotional resilience throughout my life. I recommend everyone finds out more about mindfulness.

Mindfulness enables you to step out of automatic pilot and become fully present in your everyday life which improves your mental health and physical well being.

Over time, mindfulness brings about long-term changes in mood and levels of happiness and well-being. Scientific studies have shown that mindfulness not only affects the brain patterns in a positive way, it can also prevent anxiety and depression.

Mindfulness teaches you to observe any thoughts as they come and go like clouds in the sky. With practice, you understand that thoughts and feelings, including negative ones, are transient. They come, and they go, regardless, and ultimately, you do have a choice whether to act on them or not.

A good mindfulness practice involves adopting a neutral attitude toward one's experiences in the present moment. It invites you to pay attention and observe clearly what is happening in your life. It will not eliminate life's pressures, but it helps to cultivate a new awareness. Over time, this strengthens emotional resilience, helping you to recognise and step away from negative habits.

Here I am eighteen months on and I am still grieving but I am learning to grieve mindfully. I am learning to stop judging myself and be patient with the process. I am learning to trust that all is well and to stop striving. I am accepting and letting go. Life is good; maybe not as good as it was when Matthew was around - but I'm working on it!

We do experience special moments like the other day in the music room when Bill was editing some music on his Mac computer. We were laughing and joking about something and I said, *"If Matthew could see us laughing and joking now he would be very proud of us eighteen months on."* Just as I said this, we both got a real sense of his presence. Bill has had a few moments like this in the music room where he's experienced Matthew's presence. Matthew spent many hours in here writing and recording his songs. It was a special place for him, so it's no wonder that we feel his connection more so in here.

I know Matthew is in a place of pure unconditional love, that same infinite consciousness energy I experienced on the beach. I am so very grateful for that experience and many others which, for me, confirm that all is well.

The physical illusion of this world has fallen away like a jigsaw puzzle for Matthew and he has returned to oneness. His short life in this world was just a tiny blip of who he truly is, and he will now see his beautiful magnificence. He will now be in his fullest potential. Knowing this helps to ease the experience of grief but it doesn't take away the human emotions. I still question if I will ever be completely happy again in this physical world now Matthew has graduated before me. I do get moments of peace and bliss and in these moments, I do feel Matthew is close. In time, these moments will blossom and add more colour and happiness into my life. It will happen in my time and I welcome them in.

For now, I am at peace with where I am. I appreciate that *now* is all we really have and that everything is unfolding as it should.

I used to think that time was a healer, but I've realised now that we are the healers and that time is just the vehicle that takes us on that journey.

Two years on, five years on, ten years, twenty years on, or however long my journey is in this physical body, I will do my best to make every moment count.

One day this illusion for me will fall away like a jigsaw puzzle and my physical body will die. I will experience my true consciousness in all its glory. Until then I will use all the tools I have to be the best person I can be.

An Uplifting Ending:

Turning my grief and loss experience into something positive is the way forward for me now. I have survived the worst period of my life and my experience has taught me many lessons which I would like to share with others.

As a society we need to educate people on how to be around grief and eliminate the clumsiness and unease that currently exists. It's time to stop hiding grief behind closed doors and start talking more openly about it and encourage people to come together and share experiences. Create safe places where people can acknowledge their pain and loss, where it will be received with love and empathy, instead of awkwardness.

It's not about fixing people or forcing the healing process; it's about being there, listening and supporting because grief cannot be fixed or healed. Grief can only be absorbed, carried, experienced, loved and cared for.

It is possible to mourn your loss but still feel fulfilled at the same time knowing that life can be meaningful and happy again. It is okay to move forward in life in a positive way and still grieve. It is possible to make peace with grief.

When you make peace with pain and suffering, you are more able to connect to the good memories you have of your loved ones. These good memories are the gifts they have left behind for you to keep. This enables you to continue to have a healthy connection with them which over time, can blossom into something beautiful.

Understand that this time, space, reality is really only an illusion and all that exists is oneness and love.

Believe it, feel it, live it, love it.

Should I have kept my dignity and stayed silent?
I will let Matthew have the last word on that.

Excerpt from Matthews blog. - David Bowie's Dignified Death – And Why It Made Me Question Myself.

Before all this, I saw everything in such black and white. Every opinion came so easily. But I'm not so ignorant now, thankfully. I'm not always right, and not everything is black and white.

And I prefer it this way. It's one of the positives to come from this, I think, to have the ability to know what's important and take a step back in a situation before acting. To see things from other people's perspectives and know that everyone is fighting their own secret battle, and to not judge them without knowing all the facts.

I like to think it's having that attitude – and not the decision on whether to go public or not – that defines whether someone has dignity or not. To not just be worthy of honour or respect yourself – but to value, honour and respect the people around you, too.

Matthew Bates RIP
www.matt-bates.co.uk

Gratitude Pages:

When our son Matthew became ill, it seemed that everyone we knew wanted to help in some way. My husband Bill, our daughter Sarah, and myself would like to say "THANK YOU" to everyone who organised a fundraising event, baked a cake, brought a raffle ticket, played football, donated prizes, ran a race, sung a song or helped in some way which contributed to supporting Matthew.

The financial strain that Matthew's illness put on our family was unimaginable. We were emotionally and financially on our knees and we seriously considered selling our house to pay for anything that might help Matthew recover. My business went downhill fast as I put Matthew first in order to support him – any mother would have done the same. For a while, financial help came in the form of credit cards.

It is difficult to put into words how grateful we are for all the fundraising. The money raised helped to pay for our hotel bills while Matthew underwent treatment at the Christie's cancer hospital in Manchester and helped pay for a huge number of daily supplements, weekly organic vegetable boxes, juicing machines, lots of specialist treatments and equipment, therapists, car parking, consultation fees, a private Oncologist, petrol costs, etc.

Special thanks must go to the AJAX TO AJAX lads: Sam Canty, Matthew Wells, Joe Weston and Joe Burns who were close friends of Matthew. They shared a love of Central Ajax in Warwick - the football club that brought them together as kids and reunited them when they coached the club's youth team.

Sam Canty understood how incredibly difficult it was

for us financially and he initiated and organised a massive fundraising event to support Matthew and our family.

The event started with a charity football match on Easter Monday between Ajax Youth 2011-13 XI and a Matt Bates XI at the Central Ajax ground in Warwick. It included a raffle, an auction and a cake sale. After the match, Sam Canty, Matthew Wells, and Joe Weston started their 430 mile bike ride, a five day ride that took them through France and Belgium, and onto Ajax Amsterdam Football club in the Netherlands. Sam, Matt and Joe were ably assisted by Joe Burns who drove the support van, and Matthew Canty and Matthew Crowther who filmed the journey for the Ajax To Ajax documentary. It was one of Matthew's wishes that the film should still be shown after his death and it was premiered in the local cinema. The documentary gives a great insight into Matt's thoughts and feelings, along with those of his friends and family.

The documentary film was made to highlight the Ajax to Ajax fundraising effort, but it was so much more than that; it also shows how friendships and how the wider community and how people we didn't even know came together for Matthew and for our family. The documentary gives an insight into Matthew's journey through cancer, but also highlights how his experience rippled out into the wider community and created an outpouring of love and support.

Thank you to Sam Canty for initiating this fundraising especially as it had a snowball effect with other people then starting their fundraising events too.

One of the many donated gifts for the Ajax to Ajax event included a limited-edition print of Pele which had been signed by the great man himself raised an amazing £650 – Thank You Castle Galleries, Leamington Spa for donating this and to Vince Canty & Patrick Lennon for sorting it out.

Total Ajax To Ajax fundraising reached a massive £16,000.03 by 293 contributors.

MUSIC FOR MATT FUNDRAISING CONCERTS

Special thanks must also go to our local music community. Our good friend Keith Donnelly contacted a number of folk clubs and asked them to support Matthew under the heading of, *Music for Matt.* Keith is an amazing character and we thank him so much for his support!

TUMP FOLK CLUB

The Tump Folk Club is based at The Humber pub in Coventry and is run by our friend Karen Orgill. Anna Ryder accompanied Keith Donnelly (and Bill) with floor spots from Matthew Powell and Rob Oakey. Thank You to everyone who played and contributed!

STOCKTON FOLK CLUB

On Tuesday 29th March the lovely people of Stockton folk club put on a gig for *Music for Matt.* As well as "Away With The Fairies" there was the great Norman Wheatley from Warwick Folk Club, Rik Middleton, "NUNC" (Geoff Veasey and his niece, Flossie) Dan Gascoigne and a cast of hundreds. Stockton Folk Club is run by a cracking bunch of people and we would like to thank them and all the people who donated. Colin, Mike, Rod, Frank and all the people who run the club are an amazing bunch! Thank You.

The Sly Old Dogs are a group of fine musicians who play Irish and Scottish music throughout the Midlands. Our mates Bob Brooker and Pete Willow decided to dedicate their gig at the Wood Farm Brewery to the *Music for Matt* appeal. It is humbling to think that those people in the audience – some of whom had no idea who Matthew was – were willing to contribute! Thank you to Bob and Pete, all those who played and to everyone who contributed!

BEDWORTH FOLK CLUB

Bill has been a regular performer at Bedworth Folk Club and Bedworth Folk Festival and we were not surprised when Malc Gurnham and Gill Gilsenan agreed to put on a *Music for Matt* night – they are very special people and we love them to bits. Performing on the night were Anna Ryder, Noel LeLong, Bob Brooker, John Kearney, Brian Phillips, Phillip Benson, Malc Gurnham, Geoff Veasey, and John Richards. Thanks to Brenda Gurnham for doing the door and raffle and scoring the quiz which was won by the Stanleys who added their £25 cash prize to the evenings funds! I am also pleased to say that Matt and Bill were able to pop in for a short while. Thank You so much to everyone who played, organised the event and contributed to the evening.

WARWICK FOLK CLUB

Thanks goes to Norman Wheatley who dedicated Monday 18th April 2016 to the *Music for Matt* fund. Performing was Keith Donnelly, Martyn Oram, Anna Ryder, Flossie Malavialle as well as support from Rik Middleton, Alkevan and MC'd to perfection by Micheal Luntley. It was a wonderful night and the room was packed with standing room only! Thank You All!!! Despite Matthew being very ill he insisted on popping in to say thank you to everyone and made an off-the-cuff speech.

MONTHLY FOLK CLUB AT NAILCOTE AVE

While at the Warwick Folk Club event someone popped

a cheque into my hand and asked me to give it to Matt. I'm not allowed to say who it was from – but thanks DD!!

JUSTIN'S OPEN MIC

Bill played a few songs at Justin's Open Mic at The Liberal Club Oaken House in Leamington Spa on 1st May 2016 and the club donated funds to *Music For Matt* – cheers Justin Archer and to everyone at The Liberal Club... Thanks to Dave Cook for playing too! Thanks everyone – and it's a great Open Mic too!

BANBURY FOLK CLUB

Bill has performed at the Banbury Folk Club and Banbury Folk Festival for many years and the people there are very special. Derek and Mary Droscher are amazing people and those that attend the club are all so friendly. On the 4th May 2016 they put on a special *Music For Matt* evening with Keith Donnelly leading the night together with Malc Gurnham and Gill Gilsenan, Martyn Oram, Paula and Stuart Tindall and Linda Watkins all performing (not forgetting Richard Watkins on the sound) – which made it a pretty damn good line up! Thank you to everyone involved – Bill never had so many hugs in such a short space of time!

LIVERPOOL HALF MARATHON

Our family friend and superstar Ursula Holden Gill kindly ran the Liverpool Half Marathon on Sunday 13th March 2016 to support Matthew's appeal. Ursula – an actress, musician and storyteller – has done loads of fundraising over the years for lots of great causes. We couldn't resist heading up to Liverpool for the race and surprising Ursula with our support. We spotted Ursula around the twelve-mile mark.

It was a great moment for all of us. Incredibly, she smashed her £500 target, raising £3,270 – an amazing achievement.

Thank you so much Ursula!

THANKS AGAIN

Contributions to the Ajax to Ajax fund raising page and Ursula's Half Marathon page includes donations from… Bernard & Sue Gallagher, Charles Maynard, Georgina Fitton, Stella and Te, Nan Hickerton, Sean Lonergan, Alicia, Sinead Gately, Tim Goundry, Anneka Noon, Freddie Wright, Jenni Stac, Mike and Kate Devereux, Luke Ayris, Ellie Rowley, Tom Devereux, Callum Madden, Darren Feeney, Rob Griffin, Ben Robinson, Lisa Murphy, Claire Burdett, Nikki, Pete, Luke, Matthew & Hannah, Josh Geddes, Kai Geddes, Kath Geddes, Sophie Johnson, Nicky A, Julie & Guy Filhol, Jamie Ciampa, Kirsty, Lisa Poulton, Vince Humby, Sian Javadi, Steve Cooper, Jonathan Handford, Kevin De Byrne, Jim & Joy Barry, Mike Atkinson, Gaz Manley, Nan Hickerton, Nicola Brewster, John & Jackie Patterson, Ellie Molyneux, Kat Turner, Clare O'Reilly, Pam Ellis, Chris & Mick Lucey, Olivia – Vogue International, Ann & Leon Sayce, Rebecca Shaw, Sally & Brian Young, Arthur & Megan, Sam & Louise Weston, Sam Wanless, Lou & Rich, Dave O'Driscoll, Win & Arth, Jules Wells, Betty Campbell, Maureen Hobson, Dave & Vel Johnson, Cassie and Tina, David & Hayley Fitchett, Ben and Helen, Alice Earley, Lesley Bevan, Maidy, Aillie & Duncan, Sophie and Adam Lewis, Claire Latham, Lucy and Bob, Penny Haynes, Martha & Joe, Danny and Amanda Mckendry, Dave Matthews, Dave & Sarah, Emma, James Purcell, Ellie, Helen Mulkeirins, Michael Thomas, Pa, Eamon & Debbie, Lucy-Meg, Yvonne Hammond, Fiona Crowther, Nicholas Rogerson, Daniel Bate, Will Pendred, Anne

Warren, Joanna Clifton, Shirley Welsh, Heather O'Sullivan, Aliki Marcopoli, Emma Davis, Alistair McCartney, Tommy & Treena O'Reilly, Dave & Jackie Gregory, Phillip Brown, Becky and Mikey, Jess and Chris, Olivia Meguer, Campbell McKee, Dave Rogerson, Elaine Harris, George The Monk, Martin Day, Muttley Wells, Eleanor Carne, Nicole Dudley, Hazel and Andrew, Gill and James, Richard Hoyland, Mark and Katrina Crawford, Monica Clifton, Lisa and Da, Ann Glendon-Doyle, Jen Dulson, Patrick Mulligan, Amelia Gallini, Mary Cannon, Alex Chamberlain, Matt and Claire Roberts, Janet, Win and Arth, Jules Wells, Charles Mcallen, Katrina Mason, Sacha Sutton, Daniel Ciampa, Wendy Horley, Caroline Endersbee, Claire Elsworth, Sarah Reader, Helen, Aaron Satchwell, Jack Keeling, Ami Paneser, Mike Govier, Bernie, Ellen Goodwin, Katie Swindells, Charlie Owen, ITALPIZZA srl Italy, Verity Castle, Pete and Liz, Clare Twycross, Scott Davis, Clara Mã©ndez, Joe Hewison, Stewart & Jane Payne, Ian & Fiona Salmon, Margaret Pattenden, Linda O'Sullivan, Mich Handford, Hank & Jean Handford, Liam Moody, Emmie, John & Carol Canty, Ollie Stuchbury, Theresa Mansfield, Rebecca Lonergan, Malyon family, Laura Ellis, Ben O'Driscoll, Kyle Ball, Sue, Antony Lewis, Sue & Ted, Jay Scriven, Dan Wickes, Dorothy Bigley, Joe Yeates, Sarah Rudge, Chris and Claire, Sonya Heesom, Lorraine Goor, Rachel Law, Steven Aspinall, Vicki Street, Alex and Andy Hickerton, Chrissie Hickerton, Rebecca Cleveley, Barbara Greewal, Dan Brown, Hattie Fellowes, Marina & Bruce, Jacky & Pete, Ruth Males, Mike & Sarah, Monica, Richard and family, Jake McCarthy Phillips, Oliver Canty, Anne Peet, Jon Byrne, Joe Canty, Jane Fellowes, Wendy Ann Williams, Andrew Burridge, Tony Conway, Ryan Timms, Silvia, Tim Micallef, Jack Telford, Graham Binks, Sarah Empson, James Geddes, Ol and Family,

Liam Salmon, Niki O'Connell, Gina Creese, Kath and Ian Montgomery, Sonya Heesom, Mel Timms, Christian, The Hoffs, George Keaney, Matt, Shaun Ellis, Harry Conway, Sinead Cannon, Lucy Cook, Paul & Glen Elliott, Kelvin, Thomas Callaghan, Matt Barratt, Kathy Field, Luke Young, Jon Harrington, Mum, Alan Harvey, Nikki Jones, Vince & Chris, The Sherman Family, Lucy, Auntie Pat, Andrew, John Wright, Heidi Kharbhihm, Diane Caroline and Callum,, Robin and Gill Kaye, Christine Murray, Chris and Pete, Fiona Henderson, Jonathan Waller, B and L Rowley, Nick Broomfield, Jane Hostler (Gallagher), Annie Heawood, Martin and Lisa Bradbury, Lisa Hall, Katherine, Karen Turner, The Meguer Clan! Charlotte Richardson, Kay and Pete Bonehill, Liz & Chris, John Neal, Chris Pat & Hannah, Peter Delves, Ian & Sue Hartland, Geoff Phipps, Rupe, Chris & Jenni Barthakur, Lynn Owen, Ian Bland, Just Grilles, The Cox Family, Justin Archer, Dave Page, Linda & Richard, John Kearney, Pete & Chele Willow, Mick and Carol Dolby, Bob Brooker ... and many, many others!!!!!

ANONYMOUS DONATIONS

There were also a large amount of anonymous donations and although we don't know who you are we would like to say a massive Thank You to you all. Some donated through the Ajax To Ajax funding page, others donated via Ursula's funding page and others put money into an envelope and popped it though our letterbox (we would have loved to say thank you to your face over a cup of tea). We can guess who some of you are – and we definitely know who others are – but they have asked to remain anonymous.

There have been others who have constantly helped our family. Sonya Heesom (my bestie) was amazing and often turned up out of the blue with groceries. Keith Donnelly came to record at our music studio on more than one occasion and ended up just listening to Bill talking and somehow, he still managed to make him laugh (Keith has been amazing). Anna Ryder also recorded an album at our studio and proved to be a great listener (as well as being an incredible musician and songwriter) and it's no wonder that her CD took so long to come out, she had to put up with Bill blabbing! Our friends Stewart and Jayne have always been amazing (we drank the wine Stewart – thank you!), Kevin & Wendy have been great friends and so have all Bill's colleagues at work especially his amazing boss.

Also… P.G, O.R, B.G …. you know who you are!

TOY SALE

Maddie sold some toys to help her Cousin Matthew and raised £18.17 – what a smasher!!!!

GOWER COTTAGE BROWNIES

Kate (my cousin) from Gower Cottage Brownies kindly donated a hamper to Matts appeal! For the best brownies ever, check out her website. www.gowercottagebrownies. co.uk - Thanks Kate!!!

A huge thank you to Lesley Smith, and all her colleagues at Warwickshire Council offices. They raised £220 with donations to her raffle. Thank you, Lesley!

The love and support from relatives, friends and the wider community kept us going and we will be eternally grateful for each and every one of you. You made Matthew's remaining time on this planet so much more comfortable and we will never forget you for that. Thank you sooo much. xxxxxxxxx

<u>Total money raised by combining all fundraising events reached £25,230.94</u>

After Matthew passed away, the remaining fund money paid for his wake at Stoneleigh Abbey. It was an incredible celebration of Matthew's life, surrounded by everyone who knew and loved him. We were able to give him a great send off because of the generosity of these people. Thank you.

Thanks also to Dr Manning from Starthrowers - The purpose of Star Throwers is to guide and support those who wish to look at all aspects of cancer treatment either before or after treatment with conventional therapy and also give advice on the prevention of cancer in those at high risk. Dr Manning went the extra mile for Matthew and we will never forget the hope he gave us when we were told there was no hope. www.starthrowers.org.uk

Thank you also to the staff and practitioners at the Kenilworth chiropractic clinic in Kenilworth. They were extremely generous with their time and their support for Matthew and he received great care and attention from amazing people. www.kenilworthchiropractic.com

Our thanks also to the wonderful medical professionals who went the extra mile for Matthew. We did get to see the best and the worst of the NHS but we choose to remember the special individuals who really cared.

- The Christie hospital in Manchester never gave up on Matthew and we will always remember their kindness and positivity.
- The nursing staff at Coventry and Warwickshire Hospital (you know who you are) and all the staff in Warwick Hospital especially Mary Ward and the A&E Department.

- The community nursing team. Their visits to our home were always supportive and caring and we were so pleased that Matthew experienced excellent nursing during this time.
- Thank you also to the Myton Hospice for making Matthews last five days on this planet as comfortable as possible.

There truly are angels here on earth.

Emotional Freedom Techniques (EFT)
- Tapping Therapy

Throughout this book I often mention various techniques that I use in my complementary practice, which have become an invaluable tool to help me get to where I am today. These include a tapping technique, also known as Emotional Freedom Technique (EFT) and Matrix Reimprinting.

EFT is a constantly evolving technique of which there are many variations, but it is commonly known as Tapping Therapy.

Essentially these techniques address the entire mind/body system which include what you think and how you process your thoughts, emotions, beliefs and past experiences along with how your body responds.

It is a simple but very effective technique which has the potential to release trapped emotions and even clear years of emotional baggage. This became an invaluable tool which helped get me to where I am today. I also worked with other practitioners who guided me in a safe way.

I had to be ready to work with this technique because in the early day days when grief was very raw, I didn't want to do anything. I wanted to sit in my emotion and feel everything. It is important to allow yourself to experience the rawness of grief and not try to change anything until you feel ready. EFT is a very transformational technique and grief cannot be rushed.

Matrix Reimprinting:

Matrix Reimprinting is the evolution of EFT.

The theory behind Matrix Reimprinting is that our unconscious minds are all connected through what we call the Matrix or the Field: an understanding common to many philosophies and cultures. The Matrix is a quantum dimension which holds all our individual selves, past, present and future. We call these selves, ECHOs (Energetic Consciousness Holograms). Once in the Matrix, which we can access using past traumatic events as a gateway, we can communicate with other people, including our loved ones who have passed over.

Working with Matrix Reimprinting enables us to re-visit past traumas and events and interact with our ECHOs. We cannot change our past or what's happened, but we can change how we perceive past events, resolve the trauma and change our perception of these negative memories.

By connecting and communicating with our ECHOs, we are able to understand the decisions we made at the time and create more resourceful interpretations. Together we can generate new pictures and new feelings which create new positive emotions. We can also work with our future ECHOs too.

I was holding onto some very painful memories I had of Matthew regarding his two years of illness, his treatments, experiences and traumas and his death. These were memories I couldn't even talk about without becoming deeply distraught. Matrix Reimprinting allowed me to gently re-visit these dark memories and, in doing that, I connected with my son.

Matthew popped into the Matrix time after time,

reassuring me he isn't suffering now. Each time, I could see his smiling face reminding me that he isn't there any more in that memory. Each time we connected, he would say, "Come on Mum, you know this stuff. Why are you hanging onto it? Let it go. I'm not there now." To see him looking so peaceful and happy and to hear his voice gave me great comfort.

I healed the most painful memories easily and in such a short amount of time, which to some people, would seem impossible. And by knocking out the negative emotional intensity of the big ones, lots of other painful memories just collapsed too.

When I think of those memories now, I see Matthew's smiling face, I hear his voice reassuring me, and I know he is transformed, and so am I.

Imagine you could travel back in time and have a conversation with your younger self. What would you say? The Matrix Reimprinting process allows you to do this. Imagine you could travel into your future too. The Matrix or Field is a place of unlimited potential, as I discovered through my own experiences.

Some people may say I imagined my experiences or that it is just fluffy whoo-hoo nonsense, but it was real for me and it made a massive difference in how I experienced my grief journey and, in the end that's all that matters. Whatever works for you is the important thing; everyone's grief is different and different things help different people.

Matrix Reimprinting and other types of tapping therapy are not the cure for grief, because there is no cure. What these techniques did for me, was to help cultivate a different kind of relationship with my son. It allowed me to feel the connection with Matthew which reassured me that he is in a good place and all is well. It also took out those intense overwhelming feelings that come with grief and it helped me to become more emotionally resilient.

It gives me a warm feeling inside to know that I have this deep connection with my son and, although I still miss his physical presence dreadfully every day, I am grateful for Matrix Reimprinting and the various forms of EFT for making that connection happen.

Safety Page:

This exercise is not the cure for grief because there is no cure, but I do find it calms the pain inside. I still practise this exercise but some days I don't and that's fine too. I appreciate that what I resist - persists but I am still learning to love the connection, even when it hurts. It is okay, and it is safe to feel the emotion. There is always a gift or a lesson in there somewhere.

Grief can be the garden of compassion. If you keep your heart open through everything, your pain can become your greatest ally in your eyes search for love and wisdom. Rumi

If you find you are being triggered by the words in this book, please find a therapist who can support you in your transformation and healing. I have some helpful links at the back of this book.

Exercise:
- Notice the feeling (emotion) inside.
- Do not label the feeling, for example, sadness, pain, sorrow, heartache, etc. Just notice the sensation. Your mind will start looking for references to remember other times when you felt this feeling or sensation. The mind wants to make sense of this information and by connecting with a similar feeling or sensation it gives it more power. Do not allow your mind to take over. Keep yourself in the present moment. Notice your breath and tune into the feelings. Really connect to your body.

- Where is the feeling? Is it in your chest, your tummy or somewhere else?
- How big is the feeling on a scale of one to ten, with ten being the most intense?
- How does it feel? Observe it but do not give the sensation a label.
- Can you visualise the feeling inside? Does it have a colour?
- Place both your hands on your heart and take three deep breathes in and out and tune into your feeling.
- Now speak to your body, *I allow this feeling inside, I love you, you can stay as long as you like, thank you.*
- As you breathe deeply in and out, send love to the feeling inside. Imagine the feeling inside is like a small child. Allow it to feel welcome. Offer a virtual hug to this feeling.
- Know that this feeling inside is a link to the love you shared with your loved one. The pain of grief is proof you loved.
- You may find, after a while, the feeling may shift and move or completely transcend.
- You may get an insight, an uplifting message or an inner knowing that all is well.

Sometimes we just need to feel it and not fight or resist it.

Resources:

www.letterstomatthew.co.uk
www.matt-bates.co.uk
www.energyeft.com
www.matrixreimprinting.com
www.delves.co.uk
www.emofree.com
www.divinerealisation.co.uk
www.starthrowers.org.uk
www.pennybrohn.org.uk
www.trewfields.com

Culbone Trust

Check out more musings from Sarah Bates: www.sarahandthestrange.com

If you or someone you know has been diagnosed with cancer or any other scary diagnosis, I recommend the following books.

- The Cancer Revolution. Integrative Medicine. The Future Of Cancer Care. Yes To Life. Patricia Peat with thirty-seven expert contributions.
- Say No To Cancer. Patrick Holford.
- Everything You Need To Know To Help You Beat Cancer. Chris Woollams.
- Do You Want To Know What We Did To Beat Cancer? Robert Olifent.
- Chris Beat Cancer, Chris Wark

Please do not limit your healing by relying just on the conventional medical system. Read the above books and support yourself by eating the right foods and drink plenty of healthy water. Exercise and educate yourself. Follow other people who have healed themselves and find out how they did it. Be that exceptional patient. Confound your doctors. Never give up. Believe in miracles. Never lose hope, never! If it is a scary diagnosis, know that it is possible to go into spontaneous remission. It happens!

I would also like to add that it is okay to not to be positive. There is so much pressure when you have been diagnosed with an illness, to remain positive. It can be one of the scariest experiences you can have and the last thing you want to hear is people telling you to stay positive. I used to say, "*positivity is your best medicine*" and it is, but the pressure this creates inside can cause even more stress. It is okay to not be positive and to accept whatever feelings come up. Send them love, send them love, send them love.

I am personally not a fan of the big cancer charities. They spend a lot of the donated money on expensive advertisements and executive wages, etc.

These following small charities were extremely helpful and supportive for Matthew and our family and I would love it if you could support them in any way you can. Thank you.

- www.yestolife.org.uk
- www.togetheragainstcancer.org.uk
- www.cancer-acts.com
- www.canceractive.com
- www.starthrowers.org.uk

A Letter To My Grief:

Dear Grief,

I knew you were coming. You've visited me before but even though I knew you were coming this time, I wasn't prepared for you to do your worse. You can be brutal can't you.

Where do you come from? Where you lurking just around the corner, with the grim reaper, waiting for a tragedy to strike? Do you feed off my sadness? Do you enjoy and embrace your role? When you've done your job, will you leave me?

We have been to the darkest depths of my soul together and you have seen me at my worst. I was forced to go on this journey and you have been like super glue every step of the way. I'm through the worst of it now and I want you to know that. We have come a long way together and although you feel like the enemy, we have become old friends.

Sometimes I forget you are there and in those brief moments, I panic. How could I forget you? We have developed a close partnership even though I hated you in the beginning. You made me furious and you tried to break me. Remember those days? There was so much pain in my life and I wanted to die to escape you, but I'm still here and I'm starting to like you now.

I am broken but also mended like a mosaic. I have pieced myself back together and I feel whole again but the cement holding me together is still wet. It is drying but at my speed because I need some control. You controlled the situation for far too long and it's my turn now, but don't leave me. Please don't feel your job is done and abandon me. I am happy with this current version of me and I will continue to update myself as I move forward in my life, but I want to keep holding your hand. I don't want to lose you yet.

Is it possible to grieve the loss of grief?

Who grieves for you?

I will keep you close, somewhere safe inside and I will love you. There is a home here for as long as you want. I will nurture you and keep you safe. Thank you for being here. You are proof I loved and lost a special person. Is it wrong to start feeling grateful for you? Is that too weird? You haven't replaced my son and never will but there will always be a place inside for you. You are part of me now and I kinda like that. We can live together and share this body and experience this thing called life.

Can we have a ceasefire please and make peace with each other? I'd like that.

Dearest grief, you have bought so much into my life, please forgive me, I am sorry, thank you, I love you.

Louise Bates x

www.letterstomatthew.co.uk

CPSIA information can be obtained
at www.ICGtesting.com
Printed in the USA
BVHW071023020519
547195BV00001B/13/P

9 781982 280574